**Peterson's**

# HANDBOOK ON ESTABLISHING AN INTERNATIONAL RECRUITMENT PROGRAM

**Peterson's**

# HANDBOOK ON ESTABLISHING AN INTERNATIONAL RECRUITMENT PROGRAM

JOSEF SILNY

## Peterson's Guides
Princeton, New Jersey

$F$or my sons, Danny and Jonathan;
my mother; and Erwin

**Library of Congress Cataloging-in-Publication Data**

Silny, Josef.
    Peterson's handbook on establishing an international
recruitment program.

    1. Universities and colleges—United States—Admission—
Handbooks, manuals, etc. 2. College students—Recruiting—
Handbooks, manuals, etc. 3. Students, Foreign—United
States—Handbooks, manuals, etc. I. Title. II. Title: Handbook
on establishing an international recruitment program.
LB2351.2.S55   1988       378'.1056       87-35939
ISBN 0-87866-707-5

Composition and design by Peterson's Guides

Printed in the United States of America

10  9  8  7  6  5  4  3  2  1

For information about other Peterson's publications, please see the
listing at the back of this volume.

# CONTENTS

# ACKNOWLEDGMENTS

Thanks to Linda Heaney, President of Linden Educational Services; Gary Hoover, Director of Foreign Student Admissions, University of the Pacific; Judith Jurek, Director of International Admission, Chapman College; Frederick E. Lockyear, President of International Advisory Services; and Elisabeth O'Connell, Director of Transfer and International Admissions, University of Pennsylvania for reading my manuscript and for their very helpful comments, and most of all to my editor, Andrea Lehman, for all her help on this book.

# INTRODUCTION

While international student recruitment is not a new phenomenon, until recently it had only been practiced by a few, primarily private institutions. The 1982 Institute of International Education publication *Absence of Decision* observed, "Although the practice of recruiting aggressively for U.S. high school graduates of high quality or with special skills (especially athletic ones) is unquestioned, there is a prevailing sense that such activity is unseemly if not downright immoral when carried on overseas. Moreover, while admissions officers and high administrators everywhere have pored over historical data and demand projections for higher education from various segments of the U.S. population, very few have reviewed the evidence for segments of demand beyond their shores."

By the mid 1980s, however, university administrators began to think differently. As the number of U.S. high school graduates began to drop (a trend that is expected to continue well into the 1990s), colleges started looking for new ways to bolster their projected declining enrollments. Many started thinking of recruiting abroad, and today the number of institutions interested in recruiting foreign students continues to increase. Interest in foreign student recruitment is no longer limited to a few private institutions. In fact, colleges of all sizes (including many major public universities) and all entrance difficulties are recruiting abroad.

This handbook will help you decide whether an international recruitment program is right for your institution and, if so, will assist you in developing effective programs at the undergraduate and graduate levels.

# ASSESSING THE DEMANDS OF INTERNATIONAL RECRUITMENT

B efore any recruitment activities can begin, a great deal of preparation, in the form of institutional self-examination, must take place. Recruiting international students entails a large commitment of institutional resources, and it should be seen as an essential part of your college's total international activities. Those who are responsible for setting institutional goals must thoughtfully and deliberately examine the feasibility of a recruitment program and develop ethical policies. A recruitment plan that does not take into account all institutional interests might yield disastrous results. Similarly, a plan designed to serve only institutional interests and not student interests may create problems that far overshadow any benefits.

So in order to determine whether recruiting international students is right for your college, you have to take an inventory of the programs and mechanisms that already exist on your campus, your college's strengths and weaknesses, and the goals your college plans to achieve. Next evaluate institutional aims and capabilities in relation to the demands of an international recruitment program. Only after this careful self-analysis can you determine if international recruiting is right for you.

## What Are Your Goals?

Whether you wish to fill empty seats, improve the quality and diversity of your student body, or contribute to world peace, you have to understand *why* you wish to recruit international students and be prepared to communicate your reasons clearly and honestly to your students, faculty, staff, community, and prospective international students. In order for the program to work, everyone who can help make it work should understand the end you're hoping to obtain.

## What Institutional Support Can You Offer?

### The College Community

Having more international students on your campus will obviously have an effect on your current students (domestic and foreign), on your faculty and administrators, and on the rest of the community. What are these people's reactions likely to be? Can you involve them in planning the program? In order to recruit and retain international students, domestic students will need to be supportive, faculty and staff members will need to welcome the challenge of teaching and helping international students, and your community will need to see international students as an asset and a resource. You may have to educate them so that they support rather than hinder your program.

## International Student Advising

This is an area that needs close attention. If you plan to increase the number of international students on your campus, you will need to increase your budget to provide the necessary support services. You need to have professional and clerical staff who are sensitive to the special needs of international students and who are knowledgeable about U.S. immigration laws and regulations.

These international student advisers will have to provide newly arrived students with an orientation program that covers visa requirements, Immigration and Naturalization Service regulations on travel and employment, registration, academic advising, academic policy, housing, health services and insurance, the campus and surrounding environment, safety, social life, and a whole host of intercultural topics. These advisers also provide personal counseling and referral to other professionals; work with churches, synagogues, and other organizations to line up host families; and help students prepare to return to their home countries upon graduation. Development of this staff is expensive and time-consuming, but an effective advising staff is essential to the success of your program.

## English Language Program

Many international students need to study in an intensive English program prior to pursuing academic study. As a result, an institution with an intensive English program on its campus has a distinct advantage in recruiting. The institution could then offer admission to academically qualified students with unsatisfactory English proficiency under the condition that the student successfully complete the advanced level of the college's English language program prior to academic study. (Of course, if the admissions office will not accept completion of the advanced level as proof of proficiency, the recruiting advantage is lost.)

While establishing a complete intensive English language program may not be feasible, offering at least the advanced-level courses in English as a second language will enable you to expand your pool of qualified applicants. If you cannot offer an English program on your campus, you may want to develop an arrangement with another college or with an independent English program. If you do develop a cooperative arrangement, be sure to select a high-quality program so that you will be willing to accept completion of the program's advanced level as proof of English proficiency. Once again, you will be able to expand your pool of qualified international applicants.

## Financial Aid and Scholarships

Education in the United States is very expensive, and international students are not, for the most part, eligible for federal and state financial assistance. (A few states offer reduced rates for residents of certain countries, but these are very limited.) While there are a significant number of international students who are fully funded by their family or government, there are also many foreign students who need at least partial financial support in order to be able to study in the United States.

A very effective way to recruit undergraduate international students is to provide need-based or non-need financial aid, even on a limited basis. However, since it is virtually impossible to accurately determine the financial need of an international student, I recommend the use of non-need scholarships. An institution that is not well known abroad will be able to break into the market much faster if it can offer merit awards. In addition, even partial-tuition scholarships can help institutions improve the quality of their international student body.

However, if your institutional philosophy does not allow non-need scholarships, need-based financial aid is an alternative. Be warned, however, that determining need can be very complicated.

If you do not have or do not want to develop your own financial aid form for international students, you may wish to use the Foreign Student Financial Aid Application, which was developed by the College Scholarship Service and by the Office of International Education of the College Board. The College Scholarship Service does not process the application. Therefore, it is imperative that you work closely with your financial aid office. The international student should return the application with bank statements, tax records, and letters from parents' employers. You may also require the applicant's high school principal or faculty adviser to comment in the letter of reference on the ability of the student and his or her family to pay for study in the United States.

If you choose to award aid, packages should consist primarily of grants and part-time on-campus jobs. I do not recommend giving loans to international students, because most will not be able to repay loans and your institution will find it very difficult to collect from students once they return to their countries.

Financial assistance is even more important at the graduate level, and institutions interested in recruiting international students must be willing to offer them fellowships and teaching and research assistantships. By providing aid, an institution should be able to increase the quality and diversity of its international graduate students while ensuring a high quality of graduate teaching and research assistants.

# What Programs and Policies Do You Have and How Will They Be Viewed by International Students?

## Academic Programs

The majority of international students come to the United States to study engineering, business, and computer science. However, even a liberal arts college can be successful in recruiting international students. Knowing how attractive your programs of study are to international students is important, but so is marketing your programs well and taking opportunities to make them more attractive. For example, if, along with your liberal arts majors, you offer cooperative programs with other institutions, such as a 3-2 preprofessional program, foreign students may be more interested in your college. However, it is vital that preprofessional programs (e.g., engineering, architecture, or business) be accredited by the appropriate professional association. Since most countries only recognize degrees from professionally accredited programs, it will be very difficult for an institution with unaccredited professional programs to recruit foreign students for these programs.

## Living Arrangements

Institutions with housing on campus clearly have an advantage over those without it. In any case, housing on or off campus must be provided. Is housing hard to get? Is it expensive? Can you guarantee it for international students? Can you arrange for host families? International students will need answers to all these questions, and if the answer to most of them is "no" you may not find many interested foreign students.

Similarly, international students often have special dietary requirements for either religious or cultural reasons. Most needs can be met by flexibility in your meal policy, by furnishing kitchen facilities in the dormitories or on-campus apartments where students can cook for themselves, or simply by having a food service that offers such options as vegetarian or kosher cooking, serves a variety of fresh fruits and vegetables, and provides bread and rice with all meals.

## Admissions Requirements, Procedures, and Policies

Admissions requirements and procedures deserve very close scrutiny, because they can be either very effective tools or hindrances to an effective program of recruitment. The international students you recruit should be of the same academic quality as your domestic students. If you were to recruit international students who were academically superior to your domestic students, you would probably not be able to retain them. Needless to say, you do not wish to recruit international students whose academic preparation is not strong enough for your institution.

However, in order to determine the academic quality of the international student, many institutions rely too heavily on the U.S. standardized tests, such as the SAT, GRE, or GMAT, rather than trying to understand the applicant's educational system. Flexibility is very important in admissions policies. For example, institutions that require the SAT will not be able to enroll students from the People's Republic of China because, at present, the SAT is not given there.

In reviewing your admissions policies, look closely at each procedure to determine if it is necessary and how it affects the international applicant. For example, many institutions still use a preliminary application. This procedure clearly discourages international applicants, who are more apt to apply to institutions that send them the application for admission quickly after their initial request. (You will, however, need to have a special application for international students in order to help you determine what kind of visa the applicant has or will require, what the native language is, which institutions he or she has attended, the applicant's credentials, and whether the applicant has sufficient funds to pay educational and living expenses.)

Personalization of the admissions process is very important, and form letters should not be used. When you receive an inquiry from an international student, a personalized or personal letter should be sent and all of the student's questions should be answered. Your letter should be friendly, yet somewhat formal, and students should be mailed all brochures they request. Since most international applications arrive incomplete, you should reply with a personalized letter telling applicants what information is missing and urging them to complete their file.

Faculty involvement is also important. A letter from a faculty member to a prospective undergraduate providing information about a particular field of study is very helpful. However, a faculty letter to prospective graduate students is *crucial* to an effective international recruitment program. Prospective graduate students will want to receive very specific information about academic programs, individual faculty, their professional interests, current research, facilities, and the availability of teaching and research assistantships. The ability of faculty to assume this role will be integral to the success of your program.

The final key ingredient in your admissions and recruitment effort is speed. Institutions that answer inquiries quickly and process applications expeditiously will be more successful in recruiting abroad. Mail service overseas delays correspondence enough. Unwieldy admission machines that take eternities to respond to inquiries will not yield many students.

# RECRUITMENT PLANNING

If, after reading the previous chapter, you feel you know what services and programs you will have to set up, what policies you will have to tailor, what aspects of your college will be attractive to international students, and, most important, that such a program will benefit your institution, you're ready to start planning.

A word of caution: Keep in mind that unrest in some parts of the world, weak foreign economies, the fluctuating value of the U.S. dollar, and changing policies of foreign governments make long-term planning of international student recruitment virtually impossible. The only thing one can predict about international recruitment is that it is unpredictable.

In addition, patience is an important virtue for institutions not well known abroad. Colleges that are not willing to make at least a three-year commitment to international recruitment are advised not to get involved. It will take at least that long for the overseas advisers to get to know you and to see that your institution has made a genuine commitment. Once you enroll international students and they are satisfied with your college, you will begin to receive applications from their family members and friends and from those the advisers steer your way.

## Determining International Markets

First, find out where your currently enrolled international students come from. This is your established market. Next, decide how many international students you would like to enroll, of what academic quality, and from how many countries. It is imperative that you not become dependent on one or a few countries. Having only a few countries represented does not provide a truly heterogeneous student body, and it makes your recruitment program vulnerable to factors beyond your control.

You'll want to find out where international students studying at other colleges in the United States come from, as these countries will probably provide a good market. *Open Doors* and *Profiles,* published by the Institute of International Education, give information on which countries international students come from, which U.S. institutions they attend, and which majors and levels they pursue. These publications will help you decide which countries to concentrate on. However, which countries you target will also depend on whether you are interested in recruiting undergraduates, graduate students, or both. For example, an undergraduate recruiter will not find Taiwan or Korea very productive, since the overwhelming majority of students who come to the United States from those countries are pursuing graduate study. Check all the

demographics thoroughly in order to identify the areas where you will
have the best chance of finding qualified students for your institution.

## Setting an International Recruitment Budget

An effective program for international student recruitment has to be
funded well, and you need to include in your budget the following:
highly skilled professional and clerical staff, travel, postage, telephones,
office space and equipment, publications on foreign educational
systems, stationery, special application forms, brochures, conference
participation, advertising, international student searches, and
entertainment.

Budgets can vary widely. In small institutions international student
recruitment might be handled by an admissions officer on a part-time
basis. In large institutions there may be three or more full-time
international admissions officers involved with all aspects of
international student recruitment and admissions. Institutions that are
interested in developing an effective program may wish to include in
their budget the cost of a consultation with a highly qualified
professional in the field of international admissions and recruitment.
This individual would be able to assist in developing a tailor-made
international student recruitment program and the appropriate budget.

## Producing Effective Brochures

In order to recruit international students, you have to develop a
brochure just for them. Already existing publications (such as
viewbooks), written for domestic students, won't contain all the right
information, and sending the college catalog abroad soon becomes very
expensive. Therefore an international student brochure that succinctly
covers the appropriate information is vital.

This brochure may be the only publication the prospective
international applicant receives from your institution, and it will be a key
factor in the student's decision about whether to apply. Therefore, it is
imperative that it be of high quality.

Color pictures are highly recommended. International students are
especially interested in seeing pictures of the campus, students and
faculty, facilities, and the surrounding community. However, because of
cultural and religious considerations, certain pictures that are fine for
domestic publications, such as men and women holding hands or sitting
together in a dorm room, may not be appropriate for an international
audience. Also, pictures of your football team and cheerleaders may be
seen by some students, who are not familiar with life on U.S. campuses,
as an indication that the institution is not very academically oriented.
Currently enrolled international students can help you select
appropriate photos for your brochure.

When you are preparing the text for your brochure, bear in mind that foreign students and their parents may not be familiar with the U.S. educational system, and terms such as credit, major, or semester may need defining. Since English is a foreign language for many international students, your publication should be written clearly and simply. Translation of the brochure into other languages is helpful but not necessary; most international students interested in studying in the United States have at least a basic knowledge of English. However, those institutions with intensive English programs may benefit by printing their brochures in such languages as Spanish, Japanese, and Arabic.

Be sure to cover the following topics in your brochure:

1) A statement of why you are interested in enrolling international students
2) Information about your institution: type, location, accreditation, and history. Location is especially important, and a good location can be a real recruiting advantage. Wherever your campus is, however, you need to portray its size, surroundings, and climate accurately. Whether your institution's environment is urban or rural, warm or snowy, you will want to attract only those foreign students who will be comfortable with it.
3) Academic information: majors, degrees, faculty, student-faculty ratio, average class size, library, other facilities, research, and calendar
4) Students: size of enrollment, diversity, international student services, student life and organizations, and athletics
5) Housing: on campus and off campus
6) Costs: tuition, fees, room and board, books and supplies, medical insurance, personal expenses, and summer living expenses
7) Financial aid, scholarships, and campus employment (whether available and how to apply)
8) Admissions requirements. (Specify which academic credentials and tests are required from each country; see the example on the following page.)
9) English language proficiency. (State whether you require the TOEFL or another English proficiency test.) If you have an intensive English program, describe it. Be sure to mention if you are able to offer admission to academically qualified students with unsatisfactory English proficiency on the condition that they successfully complete your English program before enrolling in the academic program. Also be sure to mention if students are able to enroll concurrently in the advanced level of your English language program and selected academic courses. International students find these options very attractive.
10) Information for admitted students: tuition and housing deposits, obtaining F-1 or J-1 visas, the nearest airport, and transportation to your campus

## Eligibility for Admission at the University of Miami

| Country | Undergraduate Admission | Graduate Admission |
| --- | --- | --- |
| Argentina | Bachillerato | Licenciatura |
| Bahamas | 5 Academic GCE "O" Level Subjects* | Honors Bachelor's degree |
| Barbados | 5 Academic GCE "O" Level or CXC Subjects* | Honors Bachelor's degree |
| Bolivia | Bachillerato | Licenciatura |
| Brazil | Certificado de Conclusao de 2° Grau | Bacharel or Licenciado |
| Canada | SSHGD, equivalent province diploma or 1st year of C.E.G.E.P. | Honors Bachelor's degree or the equivalent |
| Chile | Licencia Secundaria | Bachillerato, Licenciatura, or Título of at least 4-year duration |
| China | High School Graduation | Bachelor's degree |
| Colombia | Bachillerato | Licenciatura or Título |
| Dominican Republic | Bachillerato | Licenciatura of at least 4-year duration |
| Ecuador | Bachillerato | Licenciatura or Título |
| Egypt | General Secondary Certificate of Education | Bachelor's degree |
| El Salvador | Bachillerato | Licenciatura |
| France | Baccalauréat | Maîtrise or equivalent |
| Germany | Maturity Certificate | Diplomgrad, Staatsexamen, or Magister Artium |
| Greece | Apolytirion from Lyceum | Ptychion |
| Guatemala | Bachillerato | Licenciatura |
| Haiti | Baccalauréat Partie II | Diplôme d'Études Supérieures or Licence of at least 4-year duration |
| Honduras | Bachillerato | Licenciatura of at least 4-year duration |
| Hong Kong | 5 Subjects on Hong Kong Certificate of Education | Honors Bachelor's degree |
| India | Higher Secondary School Certificate | Bachelor's degree in Engineering or Architecture, Master's degree in other subjects |
| Indonesia | Idjazah S.M.A. Diploma | Sarjana or Insinyur |
| Iraq | Baccalauréat | Bachelor's degree |
| Israel | Bagrut | Bachelor's degree |
| Italy | Diploma di Maturita | Laurea |
| Jamaica | 5 Academic GCE "O" Level or CXC Subjects* | Honors Bachelor's degree |

| Country | Undergraduate Admission | Graduate Admission |
|---|---|---|
| Japan | High School Graduation | Bachelor's degree |
| Jordan | General Secondary Certificate of Education | Bachelor's degree |
| Korea | High School Graduation | Bachelor's degree (Taehak Taehakkyo) |
| Kuwait | General Secondary Certificate of Education | Bachelor's degree |
| Lebanon | Baccalauréat Partie II | Bachelor's degree, Licence of at least 4-year duration, or Maîtrise |
| Libya | General Secondary Certificate of Education | Bachelor's degree |
| Malaysia | 5 Subjects on Malaysian Certificate of Education | Bachelor's degree |
| Mexico | Bachillerato | Licenciatura of at least 4-year duration |
| Morocco | Baccalauréat | Licence or Ingénieur d'État |
| Netherlands | VWO or HAVO and SAT | Doctorandus, Ingénieur, or Meester |
| Nicaragua | Bachillerato | Licenciatura |
| Nigeria | 5 Academic Credits on WASC or 5 academic GCE "O" Level Subjects* | Honors Bachelor's degree |
| Norway | Leaving Certificate from Upper Secondary School | Cand. Mag. |
| Pakistan | Higher Secondary Certificate | Bachelor's degree in Engineering or other 4-year Bachelor's degree or Master's degree |
| Panama | Bachillerato | Licenciatura |
| Paraguay | Bachillerato | Licenciatura of at least 4-year duration |
| Peru | High School Graduation | Bachillerato, Licenciatura, or Profesor from a 4-year university program |
| Philippines | High School Graduation and NCEE results | Bachelor's degree |
| Saudi Arabia | General Secondary Certificate of Education | Bachelor's degree |
| Singapore | 5 Academic GCE "O" Level Subjects* | Honors Bachelor's degree |
| Sweden | Matriculation Certificate | Filosofie Kandidatexamen or Ekonoexamen |
| Switzerland | Maturity Certificate | Licence or Diplom of at least a 4-year duration |
| Syria | General Secondary Certificate of Education | Licentiate or Bachelor's degree |

*(continued)*

11

| Country | Undergraduate Admission | Graduate Admission |
|---------|------------------------|--------------------|
| Thailand | Matayom Suksa | Bachelor's degree |
| Trinidad | 5 Academic GCE "O" Level or CXC Subjects* | Honors Bachelor's degree |
| Turkey | State Lycée Diploma | Lisans or Bachelor's degree |
| United Kingdom | 5 Academic GCE "O" Level Subjects* | Honors Bachelor's degree |
| Uruguay | Bachillerato | Licenciatura of at least 4-year duration |
| Venezuela | Bachillerato | Licenciatura or equivalent |

* On the GCE, only subjects with a grade of A, B, or C will be accepted. On the CXC, only general proficiency subjects with a grade of I or II will be accepted. Nonacademic subjects such as commerce, Bible knowledge, woodwork, drafting, etc., will not be considered for admission.

## Working with Other Organizations

In order to recruit internationally you will need to work closely with major international organizations that advise international students on studying in the United States. The United States Information Service (USIS), the overseas component of the United States Information Agency (USIA), has advising centers in American embassies or consulates in most foreign countries. Some Fulbright Commission Offices and Binational Centers also offer advice on studying in the United States. Two major international organizations, the Institute of International Education (IIE) and America-Mideast Educational and Training Services (AMIDEAST) have advising centers in Latin America, Southeast Asia, Africa, and the Middle East. There are also a number of private, nonprofit educational advising centers abroad such as the Venezuelan-American Friendship Association and Association for Norwegian Students Abroad (ANSA) as well as foreign-government-sponsored organizations such as the Civil Service Commission in Thailand.

Finally, there are numerous private, profit-making placement agencies. Students use these agencies to receive the individual attention they cannot get at the very busy USIS advising centers or if they live in a city that does not have an advising center. However, one has to be very careful when dealing with private placement agencies. Since they are not regulated, they will vary from highly professional, well-trained, knowledgeable, and ethical concerns to unscrupulous and unethical agencies that charge exorbitant fees for placing students into often inappropriate programs and that may also attempt to collect commissions from U.S. institutions.

The amount of help you, as a recruiter, can receive from the advising centers depends on the individual center and its director. Some centers are insufficiently funded or do not have the staff or space to be of much assistance. The most help you may be able to receive from such a center is an orientation and perhaps some suggestions on which institutions to visit. On the other hand, if given enough notice, some advising centers will make hotel reservations, place an advertisement in the appropriate newspapers, secure a place for you to conduct interviews, make appointments for you to visit schools, and schedule interviews. However, remember that the latter will almost never happen during your first visit abroad. Only when you have proved yourself and established a rapport with overseas advisers can you expect to receive such cooperation.

Therefore an important part of your planning will be to get to know the people who staff all the centers you're interested in and to let them get to know you and your institution. You may also want to take an institutional membership in any of the private nonprofit organizations involved with international students coming to the United States (e.g., the National Association for Foreign Student Affairs (NAFSA), the American Association of Collegiate Registrars and Admissions Officers (AACRAO), IIE, and AMIDEAST). Membership in these organizations is highly recommended if you wish to develop an effective recruitment program. They provide assistance with publications, workshops, conferences, and many other services.

If you are recruiting undergraduates, especially from international or American high schools abroad, you will want to establish a working relationship with school guidance counselors. They are very knowledgeable, and some may be willing to help you with trip arrangements.

# Setting Up a Comprehensive Mailing List

In order to effectively recruit abroad, you need to provide information about your institution to many different people and organizations, so you will need to develop a mailing list, including overseas advising centers, American and international high schools abroad, high schools abroad that prepare students for entrance into universities in their country but also have a tradition of graduating students who pursue higher education in the United States, English language programs abroad and in the United States, and foreign embassies and consulates in the United States. For recruiting international students at the graduate level, your mailing list should include foreign universities.

This publication provides information to start a very comprehensive mailing list. On page 28, you will find addresses of advising centers operated or funded by USIA, AMIDEAST, or IIE as well as numerous other helpful organizations, companies, and schools. For information on

13

other advising centers or foreign schools that are not listed in this publication (e.g., Heng Sang Bank in Hong Kong or Bangkok Bank), write to the USIS, Fulbright Commission, IIE, AMIDEAST, or Binational centers abroad. Also add to your mailing list the names and addresses of the high schools and universities your current and former international students attended, and keep updating your mailing list with the schools of your applicants.

Add English language programs to your list. You may wish to purchase the publication *English Language and Orientation Programs in the United States* from IIE in New York. For those institutions interested in recruiting at the graduate level, foreign university names can be found in the *International Handbook of Universities and Other Institutions of Higher Education,* published by:

> International Association of Universities
> 1 rue Miollis
> 75732 Paris CEDEX 15
> France

and in the *Commonwealth Universities Yearbook,* available from:

> Association of Commonwealth Universities
> John Foster House
> 36 Gordon Square
> London, WC1 HOPF
> United Kingdom

With a comprehensive mailing list you will be ready to make your institution visible all over the world.

## Preparing a Professional Staff

Needless to say, the success of your international recruitment program will depend greatly on the program's staff, headed by an international admissions director. In hiring and training a staff, you will need to be knowledgeable about the staff's and, ultimately, the director's major responsibilities:

1) Plan and execute a worldwide recruitment program.
2) Keep abreast of educational, political, and economic developments worldwide.
3) Represent your institution to embassies and consulates in the United States and foreign countries.
4) Communicate with prospective international students through personal, written, and telephone contact.
5) Review undergraduate applications in order to render admissions decisions.

6) Review graduate applications and make recommendations to departments.
7) Evaluate international credentials and recommend undergraduate transfer credits for academic study outside the United States.
8) Serve as an authority on U.S. Immigration and Naturalization Service regulations as they relate to the admission of international students.
9) Prepare the budget for international recruitment activities.
10) Create international admissions application forms and brochures.
11) Represent the admissions office at your institution on committees dealing with international student affairs.
12) Visit high schools, universities, overseas advising centers, and foreign government agencies worldwide.

# Understanding Ethical Recruitment

In order to be effective, it is absolutely essential that the international admissions staff members familiarize themselves with the guidelines of ethical recruitment and that they follow them carefully. Should your institution violate these guidelines, even inadvertently, your reputation might suffer irreparable damage.

The National Liaison Committee on Foreign Student Admissions (consisting of AACRAO, the College Board, the Council of Graduate Schools, NAFSA, and IIE) approved, in 1980, guidelines for ethical recruitment. The following appears in *Foreign Student Recruitment: Realities and Recommendations,* published by the College Board:

To eliminate abuses in recruitment of foreign students, institutions that recruit foreign students should:
1) Provide enough candid and pertinent information that a foreign student unfamiliar with U.S. practices in higher education may make informed academic judgments.
2) Avoid contractual agreement with agents who require fee-for-enrollment payments.
3) Develop an admissions policy for foreign students that requires admissions judgments be made by institutional personnel who rule on other admissions. This policy should be based on a system of written criteria and applied in competition with other applicants.
4) Seek a match between the needs and aspirations of the prospective student and the educational opportunities an institution affords.
5) Accept the commitment to provide effective educational opportunities for foreign students and establish appropriate

      institutional policies governing foreign student recruitment, admissions, support activities, specialized programs, and curricula.

6) Provide realistic estimates of costs for tuition, educational expenses, subsistence, and related fees, and provide estimates of the extent to which financial aid or scholarships are available to foreign students.

7) Restrict evaluation of foreign academic records to personnel who are trained and competent in interpreting these records.

8) State clearly to students admitted to English language programs the extent of commitment made for their further education in the United States.

Careful attention to the ethics of your recruiting effort will ensure that your program is respected and will help you avoid problems.

# GETTING STARTED

## Getting the Word Out
### Sending Printed Materials

Once you've created a mailing list and the international publications you need, you'll want to get these materials to as many international students as possible. Start mailing your brochures along with your undergraduate and graduate catalogs and any other appropriate publications (e.g., pamphlets describing your English language programs, departmental brochures) to all the groups on your mailing list. A cover letter highlighting your programs, scholarships, or other items of note is helpful, because most overseas advisers cannot read all the catalogs they receive.

To save on postage, whenever possible, use APO, FPO, or Diplomatic Pouch addresses; they cost the same as domestic mail. Surface mail can be used for sending materials when you do not have such an address. However, keep in mind that it may take several weeks to mail materials using APO, FPO, or Diplomatic Pouch, and it may take months using surface mail. If speed rather than cost is your concern, you may want to use airmail or a courier, but be sure you know how to use international addresses correctly.

As has already been mentioned, you also want to be ready to respond to all student inquiries quickly and completely. Students may write, call, or have test results mailed to you; whatever the contact, be ready to send a personal letter describing your institution along with your brochure and the special application. Students should be encouraged to write to you if they have any questions and to apply for admission if, after reading your materials, they feel that your institution would meet their needs. Keep names, addresses, and other pertinent information for further follow-up mailings and especially if you plan to travel abroad.

## Peterson's International Student Network

Peterson's has two publications especially designed for international students: *Applying to Colleges and Universities in the United States* for prospective undergraduates and *Applying to Graduate School in the United States* for graduate applicants. Both publications provide brief profiles of institutions and include information addressing the special needs of international students. Approximately 30,000 copies of each publication are distributed to overseas educational advising centers in over fifty countries. These publications are given free to students who are interested in studying in the United States and who fill out a questionnaire at the center. The questionnaires are returned to Peterson's, where the information is entered into a database. U.S. colleges that participate in the project may access this database and receive monthly reports and mailing labels on students who meet the criteria the institutions set. Institutions can then write directly to the students and encourage them to apply. For information on Peterson's International Student Network, contact:

Peterson's
P.O. Box 2123
Princeton, New Jersey 08543-2123
800-EDU-DATA

## Foreign Student Information Clearinghouse

The Foreign Student Information Clearinghouse (FSIC) is a project of the College Board. Institutions participate by filling out the annual questionnaire. There is no cost to the institution for participating in this project. FSIC software is available in overseas educational advising centers; students, for a fee of $7 to $15 (depending on the center), can request a list of U.S. institutions that meet their criteria. For further information, contact:

Office of International Education
College Board
1717 Massachusetts Avenue, NW
Washington, D.C. 20036
202-332-1480

## Videotapes and Slides

Many overseas educational advising centers and high schools have videocassette recorders and would be pleased to have a copy of your college's video. Different areas of the world use different systems, however, so you will have to make sure your tapes can be played by the equipment in various countries. The United States, Canada, Japan, the Philippines, and Latin America use NTSC, most of Asia uses PAL, and France uses SECAM. In addition, in Latin America you will find more Beta than VHS formats.

However, despite minor problems with equipment compatibility and clearing the videos through customs, sending a video is your opportunity to bring your campus to students who are not able to visit the United States. Because circumstances may vary, it is advisable to ask centers and high schools if they would like to receive a copy of your video before sending it.

Universities, on the other hand, are not generally interested in receiving videos from U.S. institutions. Institutions interested in promoting their graduate programs should make their videos available to advising centers.

An alternative to distributing your video yourself is to use one of the commercial organizations that distribute videos or slide shows to advising centers and high schools abroad. Before you decide which company to use, contact a few of the institutions and educational advising centers that use their services. Ask the institutions whether they are satisfied with the company and whether they plan to renew their contract. Ask the centers for their impressions: How often are video or slide presentations shown? Are students interested in seeing them? If the company provides any equipment, does it service it? Two companies that provide these services are, for video distribution:

Linden Educational Services
5612 Wilson Lane
Bethesda, Maryland 20814
301-986-5687

and for slide show distribution:

P.M.S.I.
649 South Henderson Road
King of Prussia, Pennsylvania 19406
215-265-1728

## Advertisement

Another way to reach international students is to advertise. There are a number of magazines designed specifically for the international student market. They include advertisements from U.S. institutions and are generally distributed to students through advising centers. Before using a magazine, however, do research on its circulation, its market, and its student response mechanisms. Contact some of the institutions that have placed ads with the magazine. Find out what responses they received as a result of their ads and whether they plan to advertise again. Also, contact the overseas advisers in the countries where the magazine is distributed and ask for their advice.

Perhaps the best known of these magazines is *Study in the U.S.A.* It has been in existence since 1978 and has editions for Northeast Asia, Southeast Asia, Latin America, Europe, and the Middle East. *Study in the U.S.A.* contains basic information on the U.S. educational system and admissions process as well as advertisements from U.S. institutions. It is distributed free to international students who visit overseas advising centers.

For information, contact:

> Study in the U.S.A
> 4022 Whitman Avenue North
> Seattle, Washington 98103
> 206-632-8894

Another advertising option is newspapers. Many newspapers abroad periodically publish education supplements. If you wish to target a specific country, newspaper advertising may be particularly effective. However, while educational advertising may be appropriate in some countries, it may be inappropriate in others and may even damage your reputation. Contact a local overseas adviser and ask his or her advice.

## Telex and Fax Machines

As mentioned earlier, speed is of the utmost importance in an effective recruitment program. Sending documents or other communication by mail can be slow, and using a courier is expensive. Telex machines enable you to communicate much faster, and fax (from facsimile) machines enable you to send and receive copies of documents quickly and inexpensively. Many businesses and educational establishments abroad already have fax machines, and a U.S. institution that wishes to recruit internationally will find them an invaluable tool. Be sure to list your telex and fax numbers in your publications and on your business cards.

# Domestic Travel

There are a number of organizations, companies, and foreign embassies that place students in U.S. institutions. In addition to mailing them your materials, you should periodically visit these placement specialists to provide them with firsthand information on your institution. Addresses are given in the appendix, starting on page 28.

In addition, you should visit English language programs, especially in your region. While many students who enroll in English language programs in the United States know where they will pursue further academic study, there are also students who have not yet made that decision. In addition, most full-time English programs have professionals who advise students on applying for undergraduate or graduate study, and you should try to meet with them to brief them on your institution.

Finally you should visit other schools in the United States where international students might be enrolled. They may be interested in staying in the United States for the next stage of their education. Many independent high schools enroll foreign students; you may want to visit some. Four-year-college recruiters may wish to visit two-year colleges with significant international student enrollments. According to *Open Doors,* over 12 percent of all international students in the United States are enrolled in community and junior colleges.

# Foreign Travel

While foreign travel is the most expensive way to recruit, it is an invaluable experience and is the most effective way for institutions to become known abroad. If done well, the benefits are inevitable. You can provide information on your institution directly to foreign and American students studying abroad, to counselors in educational advising centers and high schools, and to faculty at foreign universities. In addition, foreign travel gives you the opportunity to truly understand foreign educational systems, cultures, and political and economic conditions. It also enables you to follow up on your other recruitment activities.

## Your Options

Foreign travel can be done individually or with a group; both have advantages and disadvantages. Without question, individuals with limited experience in international recruitment or from institutions that are not well known abroad will benefit from traveling with an established, well-run group. Even experienced professionals from well-known colleges benefit from group tours. After all, it takes a great deal of time and energy to organize a trip. If you travel with a group, it is done for you. In addition, by traveling with a group, you can pool your money and advertise heavily. You may even receive free publicity. A well-run group will often get newspaper and television coverage. This certainly adds credibility to the group and to the participating institutions. Also, as a member of a group, you will be able to receive high-level briefings at U.S. embassies or foreign ministries. Because so many U.S. institutions have begun to send representatives abroad, many overseas advisers find it difficult to handle individual visits and prefer groups.

However, there are drawbacks to group tours. The itinerary and schedule are chosen for you, and you may have to visit countries or institutions you would not otherwise visit. Also, when you travel with a group you have very little opportunity for time alone with educational advisers, guidance counselors, or university faculty. Neither is there sufficient time for alumni contacts.

But clearly the advantages outweigh the disadvantages, and institutions unable to support both individual and group travel would benefit more from groups in most instances. Just be sure the group you travel with follows the guidelines of ethical recruitment and that the tour director is an experienced international admissions professional. The itinerary and cost of the tour should be available months before the tour is to begin. Once again, before you choose a tour, speak with people who have gone on the tour in the past for their reactions.

Perhaps the best way to begin is to contact one of the three established and professionally run tours. The European Council of International Schools (ECIS) runs tours of international and American high schools in Europe in the fall and spring. Beginning in 1988, they are offering tours of Asia. Tour directors are U.S. admissions officers who have participated in ECIS tours before, and the directorship rotates annually. For more information, write to ECIS (for address, see page 30). Or, for information on the current tour director, contact the Office of International Education of the College Board (for address, see page 18).

The College Information Exchange (CIE) Between the Americas runs a fall tour of international and American high schools in South and Central America. Like ECIS, CIE tour directors are experienced admissions officers and change annually. Since CIE does not have a permanent office, contact the Office of International Education of the College Board for further information.

Linden Educational Services runs fall and spring tours to Asia as well as tours to the Middle and Near East and Latin America. In addition to scheduling visits to international and American high schools abroad, Linden organizes and participates in university fairs (see below). As a result, Linden tour participants have access to students enrolled at *foreign* high schools and universities in addition to international and American schools abroad. For more information, contact Linden Educational Services (for address, see page 19).

An alternative to individual or group travel is participation in university fairs held abroad. These fairs are organized by overseas advising centers, overseas international schools, or profit-making organizations and provide an opportunity for foreign students to meet a number of U.S. admissions representatives. Arrangements vary from organizer to organizer. Some provide a virtual tour package, while others simply organize the fair and leave travel and hotel arrangements to the participants. Some organizers do not charge a fee for fair participation, others have a nominal charge, and some require a very high fee. (Before you decide to participate in a fair organized by a profit-making organization, it is wise to check with an overseas adviser.)

If you cannot send an international admissions officer to a university fair, you may want to be represented by well-informed alumni, faculty members on sabbatical, or your students enrolled in a study-abroad program. Most university fairs are held in the fall, but the dates and locations of university fairs change yearly. (See the list below for some annual university fairs.) Contact educational advising centers overseas for current information.

| Location | Sponsor | Date |
|----------|---------|------|
| Bahamas | College of the Bahamas<br>High Schools in the Bahamas | October |
| Mexico City | American School Foundation<br>in Mexico | October |
| London | Fulbright Commission in London | October |
| Brussels | Fulbright Commission in Brussels | October |
| Paris | Fulbright Commission in Paris | October |
| Guangzhou (People's<br>Republic of China) | Institute of International<br>Education | October |
| Hong Kong | Institute of International<br>Education and Hong Kong<br>International School | October |
| Bangkok | Institute of International<br>Education and American<br>University Alumni in Bangkok | November |
| Europe (in the city<br>of the ECIS<br>convention) | European Council of<br>International Schools | November |

# Preparing for the Trip

In order for a recruitment trip to be successful, you must do a great deal of preparation. Because of budgetary considerations, foreign recruitment trips should be planned a year in advance. Of course, political unrest or dramatic economic changes abroad can play havoc with your plans. Make sure that you do not plan visits during school vacations, final exams, or national holidays. Professional publications indicate the academic calendars and exam schedules in the countries you plan to visit; UNICEF calendars show national and religious holidays the world over. A phone call to a foreign embassy will also yield this information.

Write to the person in charge of the educational advising center in a given country six months before your trip. (If you have visited the country before, do not need much help, and have a good rapport with the person in charge, three months' notice is sufficient.)

If this is your first trip, you will need to find out how much the overseas adviser is able and willing to help you. Send your proposed itinerary to the adviser, and find out if the time of your visit is appropriate. Ask for suggestions on school visits, hotel information, which newspapers to advertise in, and which government agencies or companies sponsor students for study in the United States so you can plan to visit them. (If the overseas adviser is not able to schedule your school visits, you may need to call or write each school or ask one of your alumni to help.)

You will want to work with a very experienced travel agent to get the best flight schedule for the best price. An experienced travel agent will also inform you if you need a visa. To get one, you will need to state the

23

purpose of your trip. The educational visa category is for prospective students, and the business visa is for companies that are selling products and signing contracts with foreign companies. Therefore, in most cases, the tourist visa is the most appropriate. Again, the educational adviser can be very helpful in this area.

Travel agents can also make hotel reservations, but, if possible, ask overseas educational advisers or your alumni to make them for you, because they may be able to get educational or corporate discounts. Be sure that your hotel is conveniently located for your school visits and that it is first class. You will be meeting high-level officials and well-to-do families. The hotel you stay in reflects on the type of person you are and the institution you represent. During my first trip with a group in Hong Kong in 1980, we were booked into a poor-quality hotel in a bad section of the city. One of the tour participants invited a student and his family to meet him at the hotel. The family arrived in a Rolls Royce and, when they realized where we were staying, did not bother to stop.

If you are visiting a country where English is not the principal language, be sure to ask someone at your hotel to write down its name and address as well as the names and addresses of the schools and advising centers you plan to visit. You can use this to show to taxi drivers, many of whom do not speak English, even in countries where English is widely spoken, such as Hong Kong and Malaysia.

You will need to secure a place where you can interview students. In some cases the advising center may have facilities you can use. Otherwise, you should rent a conference room at your hotel; using your hotel room for interviews is not appropriate.

Once your itinerary has been finalized, send an invitation to meet with you to current applicants, to students who have requested applications, to students who had test scores mailed to you, and to students whose names you received as a result of your participation in Peterson's International Student Network. Send an announcement of your interviews to schools that you will not be able to visit. Also, place a newspaper advertisement announcing your interviews in countries where it is appropriate. In most cases, overseas advisers can help you place an ad; otherwise, call or write the newspaper directly.

Write to your alumni abroad and, if feasible, ask them to organize an alumni meeting during your visit. As has already been mentioned, alumni can help you make travel arrangements. They, or even parents of currently enrolled students, can also help arrange for school visits if the school you would like to visit is not cooperative.

Before you travel abroad, be sure you become familiar with the educational systems of the countries you plan to visit as well as the culture and the political and social systems. NAFSA, AACRAO, IIE, or AMIDEAST publications will provide this information. Also be sure you know how many international students your institution now enrolls, especially from countries you will be visiting.

Finally, be sure you have a sufficient number of international applications and brochures for your trip. The applications should be precoded in order to identify the students who apply as a result of your trip. Since carrying your materials, in addition to your suitcases, may be difficult and you may run into problems with some customs officials, it is best to mail your materials, by surface mail if you have enough time, otherwise by air, in care of the overseas educational centers or your alumni.

# Over There

It is very important during your recruitment trip that you visit the overseas educational advisers to receive a briefing on the country you are visiting, to provide them with information on your institution, and to answer any questions they may have about the U.S. educational system. In order for your recruitment to be successful, you must be seen not only as a recruiter but also as a valuable resource. When traveling abroad, you represent not only your own institution but also U.S. education in general.

Consequently, at every high school, university, or counseling center, you should offer to give a presentation on one or more of the following topics: the structure of the U.S. educational system, the selection of appropriate institutions of higher education, the application process and testing procedures, the cost of higher education in the United States and financial aid availability, accepting offers of admission and the preparation needed for travel to the United States, and student life on campus. This type of information is needed and appreciated abroad.

After your presentation, give students an opportunity to ask questions about your institution or any general topics. Make sure you have time to meet with guidance counselors when visiting high schools and with departmental chairpeople when visiting universities. In addition, remember that this is a learning experience for you; it is wise to take notes and keep a journal.

A very effective way to recruit is to have well-informed and enthusiastic alumni with you during your school visits and interviews. They can help if there is a language problem, and students and parents will feel more comfortable asking them questions. In addition, your alumni give you credibility. They can also contact applicants and host receptions for accepted students.

During interviews, prospective students will ask questions about your institution, including those about admissions requirements and cost. You will be presented with a great variety of academic credentials, and students will want some answers. While you cannot make admissions decisions during the interview, it is appropriate and expected that, after you have reviewed the student's academic credentials, you will either encourage or discourage the student from applying and you will provide the student with some indication of the transferability of credits from previous study.

In addition to your alumni and parents of your students, your faculty, administrators, and currently enrolled students can assist you with recruitment of international students. A number of your faculty or administrators travel abroad to do research, for conferences, or for sabbatical. Some of them will be pleased to assist you by visiting educational advising centers, high schools, and universities or to represent your school at a university fair. It is important to brief them on your admissions requirements and the educational system of the country that they are visiting. Faculty members can be especially helpful in recruiting graduate students by visiting universities, making contacts with foreign faculty, and interviewing students.

Your faculty may be happy to contact prospects, applicants, and accepted students, especially those interested in the faculty member's department. You will find that faculty and administrators are far more willing to assist you if you take care of the logistics. Since faculty members and administrators travel abroad for another reason, their trips are paid for from their budgets or other funding. If they can make the visits on your behalf during their scheduled trip, there should be no charge to your travel budget. If recruitment activities require them to spend additional days abroad, you will need to pay their per diem during their recruitment visits.

Some of your currently enrolled students can be very helpful. During January or summer breaks, they can take catalogs and application materials to their former high schools and to overseas advising centers. Guidance counselors, teachers, and educational advisers would be pleased to hear students' impressions of your institution. Many centers would be interested in having students speak at predeparture orientation. Finally, students can follow up on your prospects, applicants, and accepted students.

## Follow-Up Activities

Upon your return, write thank-you notes to the overseas educational advisers, guidance counselors, faculty members, individuals from sponsoring agencies, your alumni, and anyone else who helped you on your trip. Send a follow-up letter to all the students you met, and include any information or brochures they requested. Finally, write a comprehensive trip report and be prepared to take care of all the tasks that are the fruits of your labor. If your trip was successful, you will begin to receive plenty of inquiries, referrals from advising centers, and, ultimately, applications. Congratulations, and remember—the second trip will be even easier.

## Seeing the Results

If you have followed the steps in this book, you will be well on your way to having an effective recruitment program. It requires a total institutional commitment and may seem complex at times, but it works. My own institution, the University of Miami, has tripled its international student enrollment, increased the number of countries from which students come from 66 to 118, and significantly improved the academic quality of international students since the program was developed. With time and energy, similar results are possible for your institution.

\

# ADDRESSES

## Organizations

Agency for International Development
320 21st Street, NW
Washington, D.C. 20006
202-647-4000

America-Mideast Educational and Training Services, Inc.
(AMIDEAST)
1100 17th Street, NW, Suite 300
Washington, D.C. 20036
202-785-0022

American Association of Collegiate Registrars and Admissions
Officers (AACRAO)
One Dupont Circle, NW
Washington, D.C. 20036
202-293-9161

HARIRI Foundation
1020 19th Street, NW
Suite 320
Washington, D.C. 20036
800-422-9955

Institute of International Education (IIE)
809 United Nations Plaza
New York, New York 10017
212-883-8200

Latin American Scholarship Program of American Universities
(LASPAU)
25 Mt. Auburn Street
Cambridge, Massachusetts 02138
617-495-5255

National Association for Foreign Student Affairs (NAFSA)
1860 19th Street, NW
Washington, D.C. 20009
202-462-4811

Organization of American States
Department of Fellowships and Training
17th Street and Constitution Avenue, NW
Washington, D.C. 20006
202-789-3000

Pakistan Participant Training Program
1255 23rd Street, NW
Suite 430
Washington, D.C. 20037
800-482-4456

Partners for International Education and Training
1140 Connecticut Avenue, NW
Suite 220
Washington, D.C. 20036
202-429-0810

# Associations of American and International High Schools

Association of American Schools in Central America (AASCA)
Escuela Internacional Sampedrana
Apartado Postal 565
San Pedro Sula
Honduras

Association of American Schools in Mexico (ASOMEX)
American School of Mexico Foundation
calle Sur 136-#135
Mexico 18, D.F.
Mexico

Association of American Schools in South America (AASSA)
AASSA Regional Development Center
North Miami Campus
Florida International University
Biscayne Boulevard at 151st Street
North Miami, Florida 33181

Association of Colombian and Caribbean American Schools (ACCAS)
Union School
P.O. Box 1175
Port-au-Prince
Haiti

Association of International Schools in Africa (AISA)
Executive Director
International School of Kenya
P.O. Box 14103
Nairobi
Kenya

Department of Defense Dependents Schools
2461 Eisenhower Avenue
Alexandria, Virginia 22331

East Asia Regional Council of Overseas Schools (EARCOS)
Singapore American School
60 King's Road
Singapore 1026
Singapore

European Council of International Schools (ECIS)
21B Lavant Street
Petersfield, Hampshire, GU323EL
United Kingdom

International School Services
P.O. Box 5910
Princeton, New Jersey 08540

Maghreb Association of International Schools (MAIS)
American Cooperative School of Tunis
American Embassy/Tunis
Department of State
Washington, D.C. 20520-6360

Near East and South Asia Council of International Schools (NESA)
Executive Director
Deree College
P.O. Box 16, Aghia
Paraskevi, Athens
Greece

Office of Overseas Schools
Room 234-SA6
Department of State
Washington, D.C. 20520

# Companies

Arabian Oil Company
Education Office
1001 22nd Street, NW
Suite 720
Washington, D.C. 20037
202-223-6265

Aramco Services Company
P.O. Box 53211
MS–1096
Houston, Texas 77052

Kuwait Petroleum Corporation
(Western Hemisphere) K.S.C.
45 Rockefeller Plaza
Suite 1776
New York, New York 10020
212-307-6622

# Foreign Embassies in the United States

Embassy of Kuwait
Cultural Division
3500 International Drive, NW
Washington, D.C. 20008
202-364-2100

Embassy of Malaysia
Malaysian Students Department
1900 24th Street, NW
Washington, D.C. 20008
202-328-2770
(Branches in Chicago and Los Angeles)

Embassy of the Sultanate of Oman
Cultural Office
1717 Massachusetts Avenue, NW
Suite 400
Washington, D.C. 20036
202-387-1980

Embassy of the State of Qatar
Cultural Office
1300 North 17th Street
Suite 1350
Rosslyn, Virginia 22209
703-528-6242

Embassy of Saudi Arabia
Saudi Arabian Educational Mission
601 New Hampshire Avenue, NW
Washington, D.C. 20037
202-342-3800
(Branches in Chicago; Houston; Costa Mesa, California; and Denver)

Embassy of Thailand
Thai Student Department of Education and Culture
1906 23rd Street, NW
Washington, D.C. 20008
202-667-8010

Embassy of Tunisia
University Mission
1515 Massachusetts Avenue, NW
Washington, D.C. 20005
202-265-0066

Embassy of the United Arab Emirates
Cultural Division
1010 Wisconsin Avenue, NW
Washington, D.C. 20007
202-342-1111

# Overseas Educational Advising Centers
## Algeria
### *Algiers*

INTERNATIONAL MAILING ADDRESS:
Student Counselor (APAO)
Service Culturel
BP 549 (Alger-Gare)
16000 Alger
Algerie

APO/FPO OR POUCH ADDRESS:
Student Counselor (APAO)
USIS/Algiers
Department of State
Washington, D.C. 20520-6030

## Antigua and Barbuda
### *St. Johns*

INTERNATIONAL MAILING ADDRESS:
Educational Advisor
American Embassy
St. Johns
Antigua and Barbuda

APO/FPO OR POUCH ADDRESS:
Educational Advisor
American Embassy
FPO Miami 34054-0002

## Argentina
### *Buenos Aires*

INTERNATIONAL MAILING ADDRESS:
Educational Advisor
Fulbright Commission
avenida de Mayo 1285 (Piso 5)
1085–Buenos Aires
Argentina

APO/FPO OR POUCH ADDRESS:
Educational Advisor
Commission for Educational Exchange between the U.S.A. and
   Argentina
USIS/American Embassy
APO Miami 34034

## Australia
### *Canberra*

INTERNATIONAL MAILING ADDRESS:
Educational Advisor
Australian-American Educational Foundation
GPO Box 1559
Canberra ACT 2601
Australia

APO/FPO OR POUCH ADDRESS:
Educational Advisor
Australian-American Educational Foundation
USIS/American Embassy
APO San Francisco 96404

## Austria
### *Vienna*

INTERNATIONAL MAILING ADDRESS:
Student Counselor
Austrian-American Educational Commission
(Fulbright Commission)
Schmidgasse 14
A-1082 Vienna
Austria

## Bahamas
### *Nassau*

INTERNATIONAL MAILING ADDRESS:
Educational Advisor
USIS/American Embassy
P.O.B. N-8197
Nassau
Bahamas

APO/FPO OR POUCH ADDRESS:
Educational Advisor
USIS/Nassau
Department of State
Washington, D.C. 20520-3370

## Bahrain
### *Manama*

INTERNATIONAL MAILING ADDRESS:
Student Advisor
American Embassy
P.O. Box 26431
Manama
Bahrain

APO/FPO OR POUCH ADDRESS:
Student Advisor
USIS/American Embassy
FPO New York 09526

## Bangladesh
### *Dhaka*

INTERNATIONAL MAILING ADDRESS:
Student Counseling
American Embassy
Adamjee Court Building (5th floor)
Motijheel Commercial Area
Dhaka
Bangladesh

APO/FPO OR POUCH ADDRESS:
Student Counseling
USIS/Dhaka
Department of State
Washington, D.C. 20520-6120

## Barbados
### *Bridgetown*

INTERNATIONAL MAILING ADDRESS:
Educational Advisor
United States Information Service
c/o U.S. Embassy
P.O. Box 302
Bridgetown
Barbados

APO/FPO OR POUCH ADDRESS:
Educational Advisor
USIS/American Embassy
Box B
FPO Miami 34054

## Belgium
### *Brussels*

INTERNATIONAL MAILING ADDRESS:
Educational Advisor
Commission for Educational Exchange between the U.S., Belgium
    and Luxembourg
rue du Marteau, 21, Hamerstraat
B-1040 Brussels
Belgium

APO/FPO OR POUCH ADDRESS:
Educational Advisor
USIS/CEE/ABL
APO New York 09667

## Belize
### *Belize City*

INTERNATIONAL MAILING ADDRESS:
Educational Advisor
American Embassy
P.O. Box 286
Belize City
Belize
Central America

APO/FPO OR POUCH ADDRESS:
Educational Advisor
Belize City
Department of State
Washington, D.C. 20520-3050

## Benin
### *Cotonou*

INTERNATIONAL MAILING ADDRESS:
Educational Advisor
Centre Culturel Américain
B.P. 2012
Cotonou
Benin

## Bermuda
### *Devonshire*

INTERNATIONAL MAILING ADDRESS:
Educational Advisor
Overseas Educational Advisory Center
The Bermuda College
P.O. Box DV356
Devonshire
Bermuda

APO/FPO OR POUCH ADDRESS:
Educational Advisor
American Consulate General
FPO New York 09560

## Bolivia
### *La Paz*

INTERNATIONAL MAILING ADDRESSES:
(Center #1)
Educational Advisor
Oficina de Becas/USIS
Casilla 425
La Paz
Bolivia

(Center #2)
Educational Advisor
Centro Boliviano Americano
Casilla 20623
La Paz
Bolivia

APO/FPO OR POUCH ADDRESSES:
(Center #1)
Educational Advisor
EDX/USIS
American Embassy
APO Miami 34032

(Center #2)
Educational Advisor
BNC/La Paz
USIS/La Paz
U.S. Information Agency
Washington, D.C. 20547

### *Cochabamba*

INTERNATIONAL MAILING ADDRESS:
Educational Advisor
Centro Boliviano Americano
Casilla No. 1399
Cochabamba
Bolivia

APO/FPO OR POUCH ADDRESS:
Educational Advisor
BNC/Cochabamba
USIS/La Paz
U.S. Information Agency
Washington, D.C. 20547

## Santa Cruz

INTERNATIONAL MAILING ADDRESS:
Educational Advisor
Centro Boliviano Americano
Casilla No. 510
Santa Cruz
Bolivia

APO/FPO OR POUCH ADDRESS:
Educational Advisor
BNC/Santa Cruz
USIS/La Paz
U.S. Information Agency
Washington, D.C. 20547

# Botswana
## Gaborone

INTERNATIONAL MAILING ADDRESS:
Educational Advisor
USIS/American Embassy
P.O. Box 90
Gaborone
Botswana

APO/FPO OR POUCH ADDRESS:
Educational Advisor
USIS/Gaborone
Department of State
Washington, D.C. 20520-2170

# Brazil
## Rio de Janeiro

INTERNATIONAL MAILING ADDRESS:
Educational Advisor
Office of Educational Advising
Consulado Geral dos E.U.A.
avenida Presidente Wilson, 147 3 andar
20.030 Rio de Janeiro, RJ
Brazil

APO/FPO OR POUCH ADDRESS:
Attn: Cultural Affairs Officer
Educational Advising Office
Consulate General U.S.A./Rio
APO Miami 34030

## Belem

INTERNATIONAL MAILING ADDRESS:
Educational Advisor
Centro Cultural Brasil–Estados Unidos
avenida Padre Eutiquio, 1309
66.000–Belem, PA
Brazil

## Belo Horizonte

INTERNATIONAL MAILING ADDRESS:
Educational Advisor
Instituto Cultural Brasil–Estados Unidos
rua da Bahia, 1723
30.160 Belo Horizonte, Minas Gerais
Brazil
APO/FPO OR POUCH ADDRESS:
Educational Advisor (Counseling)
USIS/Belo Horizonte
APO Miami 34030

## Brasília

INTERNATIONAL MAILING ADDRESS:
Educational Advisor
Casa Thomas Jefferson
SEP-Sul, EQ 706-906
70.390 Brasília, D.F.
Brazil
APO/FPO OR POUCH ADDRESS:
Educational Advisor–CTJ
American Embassy
USIS/Brasília
APO Miami 34030

## Curitiba

INTERNATIONAL MAILING ADDRESS:
Educational Advisor
Centro Cultural Brasil–Estados Unidos
rua Amintas de Barros, 99
80.000 Curitiba, Parana
Brazil

## Fortaleza

INTERNATIONAL MAILING ADDRESS:
Educational Advisor
Instituto Brasil–Estados Unidos
rua Solon Pinheiro, 58
60.050–Fortaleza, CE
Brazil

## Manaus

INTERNATIONAL MAILING ADDRESS:
Educational Advisor
Instituto Cultural Brasil–Estados Unidos
 avenida Joaquim Nabuco, 1286
69.000–Manaus, AM
Brazil

## Porto Alegre

INTERNATIONAL MAILING ADDRESS:
Educational Advisor
Instituto Cultural Brasileiro–Norte-Americano
rua Riachuelo, 1257 3 andar
90.000 Porto Alegre, RS
Brazil
APO/FPO OR POUCH ADDRESS:
Educational Advisor
American Consulate
USIS/Porto Alegre
APO Miami 34030

## Recife

INTERNATIONAL MAILING ADDRESS:
Educational Advisor
USIS–Consulado Geral dos E.U.A.
rua Goncalves Maia, 163
50.070–Recife, PE
Brazil

APO/FPO OR POUCH ADDRESS:
Educational Advisor
American Consulate
USIS/Recife
APO Miami 34030

## São Paulo

INTERNATIONAL MAILING ADDRESS:
Educational Advisor (Counseling)
Departamento de Consultas Educacionais
Associacão Alumni
rua Visconde de Nacar 86
Morumbi
05.685 São Paulo, SP
Brazil

APO/FPO OR POUCH ADDRESS:
Educational Advisor
American Consulate General
USIS/São Paulo
APO Miami 34030

## Vitoria

INTERNATIONAL MAILING ADDRESS:
Educational Advisor
Instituto Brasil–Estados Unidos
rua Madeira de Freitas, 75
29.000 Vitoria, ES
Brazil

## Brunei
### *Bandar Seri Begawan*

INTERNATIONAL MAILING ADDRESS:
Educational Advisor
American Embassy
P.O. Box 2991
Bandar Seri Begawan
Brunei

APO/FPO OR POUCH ADDRESS:
Educational Advisor
Bandar Seri Begawan
Department of State
Washington, D.C. 20520-4020

## Bulgaria
### *Sofia*

INTERNATIONAL MAILING ADDRESS:
Educational Advisor
American Embassy
1 A. Stamboliski Boulevard
Sofia
Bulgaria

APO/FPO OR POUCH ADDRESS:
Educational Advisor
AM CON GEN (SOF)
APO New York 09213

## Burkina-Faso
### *Ouagadougou*

INTERNATIONAL MAILING ADDRESS:
Educational Advisor
Centre Culturel Américain
B.P. 539
Ouagadougou
Burkina-Faso

APO/FPO OR POUCH ADDRESS:
Educational Advisor
USIS/Ouagadougou
Department of State
Washington, D.C. 20520-2440

## Burma
### *Rangoon*

INTERNATIONAL MAILING ADDRESS:
American Embassy
581 Merchant Street
Rangoon
Burma

APO/FPO OR POUCH ADDRESS:
Educational Advisor
USIS/Rangoon
Department of State
Washington, D.C. 20520-4250

## Burundi
### *Bujumbura*

INTERNATIONAL MAILING ADDRESS:
American Cultural Center
B.P. 810
Bujumbura
Burundi

## Cameroon
### *Yaounde*

INTERNATIONAL MAILING ADDRESS:
Educational Advisor
American Cultural Center
B.P. 817
Yaounde
Cameroon

APO/FPO OR POUCH ADDRESS:
Educational Advisor
USIS/Yaounde
Department of State
Washington, D.C. 20520-2520

### *Douala*

INTERNATIONAL MAILING ADDRESS:
Educational Advisor
American Cultural Center
B.P. 4045
Douala
Cameroon

APO/FPO OR POUCH ADDRESS:
Educational Advisor
USIS/Amconsul Douala
Department of State
Washington, D.C. 20520-2530

## Canada
### *Ottawa*

INTERNATIONAL MAILING ADDRESS:
Educational Advisor
American Embassy
100 Wellington Street
Ottawa, Ontario K1P 5T1
Canada

APO/FPO OR POUCH ADDRESS:
Educational Advisor
USIS/Ottawa
Department of State
Washington, D.C. 20520-5480

### *Montreal*

INTERNATIONAL MAILING ADDRESS:
Educational Advisor
USIS
P.O. Box 65
Montreal, Quebec H5B 1G1
Canada

APO/FPO OR POUCH ADDRESS:
Educational Advisor
USIS/Montreal
Department of State
Washington, D.C. 20520-5510

### *Toronto*

INTERNATIONAL MAILING ADDRESS:
Educational Advisor
American Consulate General
360 University Avenue
Toronto, Ontario M5G 1S4
Canada

APO/FPO OR POUCH ADDRESS:
Educational Advisor
USIS/Toronto
Department of State
Washington, D.C. 20520-5530

### *Vancouver*

INTERNATIONAL MAILING ADDRESS:
Educational Advisor
American Consulate General
1075 West Georgia Street, 21st Floor
Vancouver, British Columbia V6E 4E9
Canada

APO/FPO OR POUCH ADDRESS:
Educational Advisor
USIS/Vancouver
Department of State
Washington, D.C. 20520-5540

## Republic of Cape Verde
### *Praia*

INTERNATIONAL MAILING ADDRESS:
Educational Advisor
American Embassy
C.P. 201
Praia
Republic of Cape Verde

APO/FPO OR POUCH ADDRESS:
Educational Advisor
Praia
Department of State
Washington, D.C. 20520-2460

## Central African Republic
### *Bangui*

INTERNATIONAL MAILING ADDRESS:
Educational Advisor/PAO
USIS
B.P. 924
Bangui
Central African Republic

APO/FPO OR POUCH ADDRESS:
Educational Advisor/PAO
USIS/Bangui
Department of State
Washington, D.C. 20520-2060

## Chad
### *N'Djamena*

INTERNATIONAL MAILING ADDRESS:
Educational Advisor
Service Culturel et de Presse (USIS)
Ambassade des États-Unis d'Amérique
B.P. 3
N'Djamena
Chad

APO/FPO OR POUCH ADDRESS:
Public Affairs Officer
N'Djamena (USIS)
Department of State
Washington, D.C. 20520-2410

## Chile
### *Santiago*

INTERNATIONAL MAILING ADDRESS:
OPEN—Oportunidades en Educación Norteamericana
Casilla 9286
Santiago
Chile

APO/FPO OR POUCH ADDRESS:
Attn: CAO
American Embassy
USIS/Santiago
APO Miami 34033

Educational materials for the following centers should be sent through the address listed above:

## Antofagasta

INTERNATIONAL MAILING ADDRESS:
Director
Instituto Chileno-Norteamericano de Cultura
Casilla P
Antofagasta
Chile

APO/FPO OR POUCH ADDRESS:
For Student Advisor BNC–Antofagasta
Attn: CAO
American Embassy
USIS/Santiago
APO Miami 34033

## Concepción

INTERNATIONAL MAILING ADDRESS:
Director
Instituto Chileno-Norteamericano de Cultura
Casilla 612
Concepción
Chile

APO/FPO OR POUCH ADDRESS:
For Student Advisor BNC–Concepción
Attn: CAO
American Embassy
USIS/Santiago
APO Miami 34033

## *Valparaiso*

INTERNATIONAL MAILING ADDRESS:
Librarian
Instituto Chileno-Norteamericano de Cultura
Casilla 1297
Valparaiso
Chile

APO/FPO OR POUCH ADDRESS:
For Student Advisor BNC–Valparaiso
Attn: CAO
American Embassy
USIS/Santiago
APO Miami 34033

## China

The following nine advising centers distribute information on study in the United States and have educational advisers available to assist students:

### *Beijing*

INTERNATIONAL MAILING ADDRESS:
Educational Advisor
Advisory Center of Foreign Educational Information
Beijing Languages Institute
Xueyuan Lu #14
Beijing
China

### *Chengdu*

INTERNATIONAL MAILING ADDRESS:
Educational Advisor
Study Abroad Training Department
Chengdu University of Science and Technology
Xingnanmenwai Moziqiao
Chengdu, Sichuan Province
China

## *Chongqing*

INTERNATIONAL MAILING ADDRESS:
Educational Advisor
Study Abroad Training Department
Sichuan Foreign Languages Institute
Shapingba
Chongqing, Sichuan Province
China

## *Dalian*

INTERNATIONAL MAILING ADDRESS:
Educational Advisor
Study Abroad Training Department
Dalian Foreign Languages Institute
Zhongshanqu Janshan Lu Jiefangjie #111
Dalian, Liaoning Province
China

## *Guangzhou*

INTERNATIONAL MAILING ADDRESSES:
(Center #1)
Educational Advisor
Study Abroad Training Department
Guangzhou Foreign Languages Institute
Beijiao Huangpodong
Guangzhou, Guangdong Province
China

(Center #2)
Educational Advisor
Study Abroad Information Service
Bureau of Higher Education of Guangzhou Province
Xihu Lu
Guangzhou, Guangdong Province
China

(Center #3)
Educational Advisor
IIE–Guangdong American Study Information Center
Ground Floor, 46-1 Dezheng South Road
Guangzhou, Guangdong Province
China

*Guangzhou (continued)*

APO/FPO OR POUCH ADDRESS:
(Center #3)
Educational Advisor
USIS/Guangzhou
FPO San Francisco 96659

## Shanghai

INTERNATIONAL MAILING ADDRESS:
Educational Advisor
Study Abroad Training Department
Shanghai International Studies University
Xi Tiyuhui Lu
Shanghai
China

## Xi'an

INTERNATIONAL MAILING ADDRESS:
Educational Advisor
Study Abroad Training Department
Xi'an Foreign Languages Institute
Wujiafen
Xi'an, Shaanxi Province
China

The following eight advising centers distribute information on study in the United States but may not have educational advisers available to assist students:

## Beijing

INTERNATIONAL MAILING ADDRESS:
Beijing National Library
Wenjin Jie #7
Beijing
China

## *Changchun*

INTERNATIONAL MAILING ADDRESS:
Jilin Provincial Library
Changchun, Jilin Province
China

## *Chengdu*

INTERNATIONAL MAILING ADDRESS:
Sichuan Provincial Library
Dongfeng Lu #222
Chengdu, Sichuan Province
China

## *Guangzhou*

INTERNATIONAL MAILING ADDRESS:
Guangzhou Municipal Library
Zhongshan Si Lu #42
Guangzhou, Guangdong Province
China

## *Harbin*

INTERNATIONAL MAILING ADDRESS:
Educational Advisor
Heilongjiang Provincial Library
Fendou Lu
Harbin, Heilongjiang Province
China

## *Shanghai*

INTERNATIONAL MAILING ADDRESS:
Shanghai Municipal Library
Nanjing Xilu #325
Shanghai
China

## Shenyang

INTERNATIONAL MAILING ADDRESS:
Liaoning Provincial Library
Shenyang Lu Erduan Wenxingly #5
Shenyang, Liaoning Province
China

## Wuchang

INTERNATIONAL MAILING ADDRESS:
Hubei Provincial Library
Wuluo Lu #45
Wuchang, Hubei Province
China

# Colombia
## Bogotá

INTERNATIONAL MAILING ADDRESS:
Educational Advisor
Comisión Fulbright
Centro Colombo-Americano
Apartado Aereo 3815
Bogotá D.E.
Colombia

APO/FPO OR POUCH ADDRESS:
Educational Advisor
USIS/Bogotá
APO Miami 34038

Educational materials for the following centers should be sent through the address listed above:

## Armenia

INTERNATIONAL MAILING ADDRESS:
Educational Advisor
Centro Colombo-Americano
Apartado Aereo 29
Armenia, Quindio
Colombia

## Barranquilla

INTERNATIONAL MAILING ADDRESS:
Educational Advisor
Centro Colombo-Americano
Apartado Aereo 2097
Barranquilla, Atlántico
Colombia

## Bucaramanga

INTERNATIONAL MAILING ADDRESS:
Educational Advisor
Centro Colombo-Americano
Apartado Aereo 466
Bucaramanga, Santander
Colombia

## Cali

INTERNATIONAL MAILING ADDRESS:
Educational Advisor
Centro Colombo-Americano
Apartado Aereo 4525
Cali, Valle
Colombia

## Cartagena

INTERNATIONAL MAILING ADDRESS:
Educational Advisor
Centro Colombo-Americano
Apartado Aereo 2831
Cartagena, Bolívar
Colombia

## Manizales

INTERNATIONAL MAILING ADDRESS:
Educational Advisor
Centro Colombo-Americano
Apartado Aereo 391
Manizales, Caldas
Colombia

## Medellín

INTERNATIONAL MAILING ADDRESS:
Educational Advisor
Centro Colombo-Americano
Apartado Aereo 8734
Medellín, Antioquia
Colombia

## Pereira

INTERNATIONAL MAILING ADDRESS:
Educational Advisor
Centro Colombo-Americano
Apartado Aereo 735
Pereira, Risaralda
Colombia

# People's Republic of the Congo
## Brazzaville

INTERNATIONAL MAILING ADDRESS:
Educational Advisor
American Embassy
avenue Amilcar Cabral
Brazzaville
People's Republic of the Congo

APO/FPO OR POUCH ADDRESS:
Educational Advisor
USIS/American Embassy–Kinshasa République du Zaire
APO New York 09662

# Costa Rica
## San José

INTERNATIONAL MAILING ADDRESS:
Educational Advisor
Educational Advising Center, BNC
Apartado 1489-1000
San José
Costa Rica

APO/FPO OR POUCH ADDRESS:
Educational Advisor
U.S. Embassy
APO Miami 34020

## Cuba
### *Havana*

INTERNATIONAL MAILING ADDRESS:
Educational Advisor
USINT
Swiss Embassy
Calzada entre L&M, Vedado Sección
Havana
Cuba

## Cyprus
### *Nicosia*

INTERNATIONAL MAILING ADDRESS:
Educational Advisor
Commission for Educational Exchange between the U.S.A. and
    Cyprus
2 Egypt Avenue
Nicosia
Cyprus
APO/FPO OR POUCH ADDRESS:
Educational Advisor
Fulbright Commission
American Embassy/Nicosia
FPO New York 09530

## Czechoslovakia
### *Prague*

INTERNATIONAL MAILING ADDRESS:
Assistant Public Affairs Officer
American Embassy
Trziste 15-12548
Praha 1
Czechoslovakia

*Prague (continued)*

APO/FPO OR POUCH ADDRESS:
Assistant Public Affairs Officer
AM CON GEN (PRG)
APO New York 09213

# Denmark
## *Copenhagen*

INTERNATIONAL MAILING ADDRESS:
Educational Advisor
Commission for Educational Exchange between Denmark and the
    United States of America
Raadhusstraede 3
DK-1466 Copenhagen K.
Denmark

APO/FPO OR POUCH ADDRESS:
Educational Advisor
Commission for Educational Exchange between Denmark and the
    United States of America
c/o USIS/American Embassy
APO New York 09170

# Republic of Djibouti
## *Djibouti*

INTERNATIONAL MAILING ADDRESS:
Educational Advisor
American Embassy
B.P. 185
Djibouti
Republic of Djibouti

APO/FPO OR POUCH ADDRESS:
Educational Advisor
Djibouti
Department of State
Washington, D.C. 20520-2150

## Dominican Republic
### *Santo Domingo*

INTERNATIONAL MAILING ADDRESS:
Educational Advisor
Instituto Cultural Domínico-Americano
avenida Abraham Lincoln No. 21
Santo Domingo
Dominican Republic

APO/FPO OR POUCH ADDRESS:
Educational Advisor
USIS/American Embassy
APO Miami 34041-0008

Educational materials for the following center should be sent through
the address listed above:

### *Santiago de los Caballeros*

INTERNATIONAL MAILING ADDRESS:
Centro Cultural Domínico-Americano
avenida Estrella Sadala
La Rinconada
Santiago de los Caballeros
Dominican Republic

## Ecuador
### *Quito*

INTERNATIONAL MAILING ADDRESS:
Educational Advisor
Comisión Fulbright
Casilla 826-A
Quito
Ecuador

APO/FPO OR POUCH ADDRESS:
Educational Advisor
Fulbright Commission, USIS
American Embassy/Quito
U.S. Department of State
Washington, D.C. 20520-3420

## *Guayaquil*

INTERNATIONAL MAILING ADDRESS:
Comisión Fulbright
Casilla 10237
Guayaquil
Ecuador

# Egypt
## *Cairo*

INTERNATIONAL MAILING ADDRESS:
AMIDEAST
6 Kamel El-Shennawy Street
Second Floor–Apt. 5
Garden City
Cairo
Arab Republic of Egypt

Educational materials for the following center should be sent through the address listed above:

### *Alexandria*

INTERNATIONAL MAILING ADDRESS:
AMIDEAST
Branch Counseling Services
3 Pharaana Street
Alexandria
Arab Republic of Egypt

# El Salvador
## *San Salvador*

INTERNATIONAL MAILING ADDRESS:
Educational Advisor
American Embassy
25 avenida Norte No. 1230
San Salvador
El Salvador

APO/FPO OR POUCH ADDRESS:
Educational Advisor
USIS/American Embassy
APO Miami 34023-0001

# Equatorial Guinea
## *Malabo*

INTERNATIONAL MAILING ADDRESS:
Educational Advisor
American Embassy
Apartado 597
Malabo
Equatorial Guinea

APO/FPO OR POUCH ADDRESS:
Educational Advisor
American Embassy/Malabo
Department of State
Washington, D.C. 20520-2320

# Ethiopia
## *Addis Ababa*

INTERNATIONAL MAILING ADDRESS:
Public Affairs Office
Educational Advisor
American Embassy
P.O. Box 1014
Addis Ababa
Ethiopia

APO/FPO OR POUCH ADDRESS:
Public Affairs Office
Educational Advisor
Addis Ababa
Department of State
Washington, D.C. 20520-2030

## Fiji
### *Suva*

INTERNATIONAL MAILING ADDRESS:
Educational Advisor
American Embassy
P.O. Box 218
Suva
Fiji

APO/FPO OR POUCH ADDRESS:
Educational Advisor
USIS/Suva
Department of State
Washington, D.C. 20520-4290

## Finland
### *Helsinki*

INTERNATIONAL MAILING ADDRESS:
Educational Advisor
America Center
Kaivokatu 10 A
SF-00100 Helsinki
Finland

APO/FPO OR POUCH ADDRESS:
Educational Advisor
America Center–USIS
American Embassy
APO New York 09664

## France
### *Paris*

INTERNATIONAL MAILING ADDRESS:
Educational Advisor
Franco-American Commission for Educational Exchange
9 rue Chardin
75016 Paris
France

APO/FPO OR POUCH ADDRESS:
Educational Advisor
Franco-American Commission for Educational Exchange
USIS/American Embassy
APO New York 09777

## Bordeaux

INTERNATIONAL MAILING ADDRESS:
Educational Advisor
American Consulate General
22 Cours du Maréchal Foch
33080 Bordeaux
France
APO/FPO OR POUCH ADDRESS:
Educational Advisor
USIS/Bordeaux
APO New York 09777

## Lyon

INTERNATIONAL MAILING ADDRESS:
Educational Advisor
American Consulate General
7 Quai Général Sarrail
69454 Lyon
France
APO/FPO OR POUCH ADDRESS:
Educational Advisor
USIS/Lyon
APO New York 09777

## Marseille

INTERNATIONAL MAILING ADDRESS:
Educational Advisor
American Consulate General
No. 9 rue Armeny
13006 Marseille
France
APO/FPO OR POUCH ADDRESS:
Educational Advisor
USIS/Marseille
APO New York 09777

## Nice

INTERNATIONAL MAILING ADDRESS:
Educational Advisor
American Consulate General
31 rue du Maréchal Joffre
06000 Nice
France
APO/FPO OR POUCH ADDRESS:
Educational Advisor
USIS/Nice
APO New York 09777

## Strasbourg

INTERNATIONAL MAILING ADDRESS:
American Consulate General
15 avenue d'Alsace
67082 Strasbourg
France
APO/FPO OR POUCH ADDRESS:
Educational Advisor
USIS/Strasbourg
APO New York 09777

## French Caribbean Department
### Fort-de-France

INTERNATIONAL MAILING ADDRESS:
Educational Advisor
Consulate General of the United States of America
B.P. 561
Fort-de-France 97206
Martinique, French West Indies
APO/FPO OR POUCH ADDRESS:
Educational Advisor
Martinique
Department of State
Washington, D.C. 20520-3250

## Gabon
*Libreville*

INTERNATIONAL MAILING ADDRESS:
Educational Advisor
Centre Culturel Américain
B.P. 2237
Libreville
Gabon

APO/FPO OR POUCH ADDRESS:
Educational Advisor
USIS/Libreville
Department of State
Washington, D.C. 20520-2270

## Gambia
*Banjul*

INTERNATIONAL MAILING ADDRESS:
Educational Advisor
USIS/American Embassy
P.M.B. No. 19
Banjul
The Gambia
West Africa

APO/FPO OR POUCH ADDRESS:
Educational Advisor
USIS/American Embassy
Banjul, The Gambia
Department of State
Washington, D.C. 20520-2070

## German Democratic Republic
*Berlin*

INTERNATIONAL MAILING ADDRESS:
Educational Advisor
USBER Box E
170 Clayallee
1000 Berlin 33
German Democratic Republic

*Berlin (continued)*

APO/FPO OR POUCH ADDRESS:
Educational Advisor
Amembassy Berlin
USBER Box E
APO New York 09742

## Federal Republic of Germany
### *Bonn*

INTERNATIONAL MAILING ADDRESS:
Educational Specialist
American Embassy
Deichmanns Aue 29
5300 Bonn 2
Federal Republic of Germany

APO/FPO OR POUCH ADDRESS:
Exchanges Specialist
USIS/Box 380
APO New York 09080

### *Berlin*

INTERNATIONAL MAILING ADDRESS:
Exchanges Specialist
America House
Hardenbergstrasse, 22-24
D-1000 Berlin 12
Federal Republic of Germany

APO/FPO OR POUCH ADDRESS:
Exchanges Specialist
USIS/USBER/AH
APO New York 09742

### *Cologne*

INTERNATIONAL MAILING ADDRESS:
Exchanges Specialist
America House
Apostelnkloster 13-15
5000 Cologne 1
Federal Republic of Germany

APO/FPO OR POUCH ADDRESS:
Exchanges Specialist
USIS/Cologne
c/o American Consulate General
APO New York 09080

## *Frankfurt*

INTERNATIONAL MAILING ADDRESS:
America House
Staufenstrasse 1
6000 Frankfurt am Main 1
Federal Republic of Germany
APO/FPO OR POUCH ADDRESS:
Exchanges Specialist
USIS
c/o American Consulate General
APO New York 09213

## *Hamburg*

INTERNATIONAL MAILING ADDRESS:
Exchanges Specialist
America House
Tesdorpfstrasse 1
2000 Hamburg 13
Federal Republic of Germany
APO/FPO OR POUCH ADDRESS:
Exchanges Specialist
USIS/Hamburg
c/o American Consulate General
APO New York 09215

## *Hannover*

INTERNATIONAL MAILING ADDRESS:
Exchanges Specialist
America House
Postfach 440
3000 Hannover 1
Federal Republic of Germany

*Hannover (continued)*

APO/FPO OR POUCH ADDRESS:
Exchanges Specialist
USIS/Hannover
c/o American Consulate General
APO New York 09215

## Munich

INTERNATIONAL MAILING ADDRESS:
Exchanges Specialist
America House
Karolinenplatz 3
8000 Munich 22
Federal Republic of Germany

APO/FPO OR POUCH ADDRESS:
Exchanges Specialist
USIS/Munich
c/o American Consulate General
APO New York 09108

## Stuttgart

INTERNATIONAL MAILING ADDRESS:
Exchanges Specialist
America House
Friedrichstrasse 23 A
7000 Stuttgart 1
Federal Republic of Germany

APO/FPO OR POUCH ADDRESS:
Exchanges Specialist
USIS/Stuttgart
c/o American Consulate General
APO New York 09154

# Ghana
## Accra

INTERNATIONAL MAILING ADDRESS:
USIS
P.O. Box 2288
Accra
Ghana

APO/FPO OR POUCH ADDRESS:
Educational Advisor
USIS/Accra
Department of State
Washington, D.C. 20520-2020

# Greece
## *Athens*

INTERNATIONAL MAILING ADDRESS:
Educational Advisor
U.S. Educational Foundation in Greece
6 Vasilissis Sofias Boulevard
Athens, 10674
Greece

APO/FPO OR POUCH ADDRESS:
Educational Advisor
U.S. Educational Foundation in Greece
USIS/American Embassy
APO New York 09253

## *Thessalonika*

INTERNATIONAL MAILING ADDRESS:
Fulbright Advisor
USIS
34 Mitropoleos Street
Thessaloniki
Greece

# Grenada
## *St. George's*

INTERNATIONAL MAILING ADDRESSES:
(Center #1)
Educational Advisor
U.S. Information Service
USIS/American Embassy
Ross Point Inn, Belmont
St. George's
Grenada

*St. George's (continued)*

(Center #2)
University of the West Indies Extra Mural Centre
U.W.I. Extra Mural Centre, Marryshow House
Tyrrel Street
St. George's
Grenada

APO/FPO OR POUCH ADDRESS:
(Center #1)
Educational Advisor
USIS
American Embassy/Grenada
Department of State
Washington, D.C. 20520-3180

## Guatemala
### *Guatemala City*

INTERNATIONAL MAILING ADDRESS:
Instituto Guatemalteco-Americano
Ruta 1, Via 4, Zona 4
Guatemala City
Guatemala

APO/FPO OR POUCH ADDRESS:
Educational Advisor
ACAO/BNCD
American Embassy
APO Miami 34024

## Guinea
### *Conakry*

INTERNATIONAL MAILING ADDRESS:
Educational Advisor
English Language School
c/o USIS–American Embassy
B.P. 12-5
Conakry
Guinea

APO/FPO OR POUCH ADDRESS:
Educational Advisor
c/o USIS
Conakry
Department of State
Washington, D.C. 20520-2110

## Guinea-Bissau
### *Bissau*

INTERNATIONAL MAILING ADDRESS:
Educational Advisor
American Embassy
C.P. 297
Bissau
Guinea-Bissau

APO/FPO OR POUCH ADDRESS:
Educational Advisor
Bissau
Department of State
Washington, D.C. 20520-2080

## Guyana
### *Georgetown*

INTERNATIONAL MAILING ADDRESS:
Educational Advisor
USIS/American Embassy
31 Main Street
Georgetown
Guyana

APO/FPO OR POUCH ADDRESS:
Educational Advisor
USIS/Georgetown
Department of State
Washington, D.C. 20520-3170

## Haiti
### *Port-au-Prince*

INTERNATIONAL MAILING ADDRESS:
Educational Advisor
Haitian-American Institute
rue St. Cyr/rue Capois
Port-au-Prince
Haiti

APO/FPO OR POUCH ADDRESS:
Educational Advisor
USIS/Port-au-Prince
Department of State
Washington, D.C. 20520-3400

## Honduras
### *Tegucigalpa*

INTERNATIONAL MAILING ADDRESS:
Instituto Hondureno de Cultura Interamericana
Apartado 201, Comayaguela
Tegucigalpa
Honduras

APO/FPO OR POUCH ADDRESS:
Student Counselor
USIS/Tegucigalpa
American Embassy
APO Miami 34022

### *San Pedro Sula*

INTERNATIONAL MAILING ADDRESS:
Centro Cultural Sanpedrana
3 calle N.O., 3 y 4 avenidas
San Pedro Sula
Honduras

## Hong Kong

INTERNATIONAL MAILING ADDRESS:
Institute of International Education
Hong Kong Arts Center, 12th Floor
Harbour Road
Hong Kong

## Hungary
### *Budapest*

INTERNATIONAL MAILING ADDRESS:
Educational Advisor
Amerikai Nagykovetsey
V. Szabadsag Ter 12
1054 Budapest
Hungary

APO/FPO OR POUCH ADDRESS:
Educational Advisor
Press & Culture
AM CON GEN (BUD)
APO New York 09213

## Iceland
### *Reykjavik*

INTERNATIONAL MAILING ADDRESS:
Educational Advisor
Iceland-U.S. Educational Commission
Box 752
121 Reykjavik
Iceland

APO/FPO OR POUCH ADDRESS:
Educational Advisor
Amembassy Reykjavik
Fulbright Office
FPO New York 09571-0001

## India
### *New Delhi*

INTERNATIONAL MAILING ADDRESS:
Educational Advisor
U.S. Educational Foundation in India
12 Hailey Road
New Delhi 110 001
India

APO/FPO OR POUCH ADDRESS:
U.S. Educational Foundation in India/New Delhi
USIS/New Delhi
Department of State
Washington, D.C. 20520-9000

Educational materials for the following centers should be sent through the address listed above:

### *Bombay*

INTERNATIONAL MAILING ADDRESS:
Educational Advisor
U.S. Educational Foundation in India
Sundeep
4 New Marine Lines
Bombay 400 020
India

### *Calcutta*

INTERNATIONAL MAILING ADDRESS:
Educational Advisor
U.S. Educational Foundation in India
8 Short Street
Calcutta 700 017
India

## Madras

INTERNATIONAL MAILING ADDRESS:
Educational Advisor
U.S. Educational Foundation in India
American Consulate Building
Mount Road–6
Madras 600 006
India

# Indonesia
## *Jakarta*

INTERNATIONAL MAILING ADDRESS:
Student Advising Service/USIS
Jalan Medan Merdeka Selatan 4
Jakarta 10110
Indonesia
APO/FPO OR POUCH ADDRESS:
Student Advising Service
USIS
Box 5
APO San Francisco 96356

Educational materials for the following centers should be sent through the address listed above:

## *Medan*

INTERNATIONAL MAILING ADDRESS:
Student Counseling
Perimpunan Persahabat Indonesia-Amerika
Jalan Imam Bonjol 13
Medan
Indonesia

## *Surabaya*

INTERNATIONAL MAILING ADDRESS:
Student Counseling
Perimpunan Persahabat Indonesia-Amerika
Jalan Raya Dr. Sutomo 33
Surabaya
Indonesia

# Iraq
## *Baghdad*

APO/FPO OR POUCH ADDRESS:
Student Counselor
USIS/Baghdad
Department of State
Washington, D.C. 20520-6060

# Ireland
## *Dublin*

INTERNATIONAL MAILING ADDRESS:
American Embassy
42 Elgin Road, Ballsbridge
Dublin
Ireland

APO/FPO OR POUCH ADDRESS:
Educational Advisor
USIS/Dublin
Department of State
Washington, D.C. 20520-5290

# Israel
## *Tel Aviv*

INTERNATIONAL MAILING ADDRESS:
Educational Advisor
U.S.-Israel Educational Foundation
P.O.B. 26160
Tel Aviv 61162
Israel

APO/FPO OR POUCH ADDRESS:
Educational Advisor
U.S.-Israel Educational Foundation
USIS/American Embassy
APO New York 09672

# Italy
## *Rome*

INTERNATIONAL MAILING ADDRESS:
Educational Advisor
Commission for Educational and Cultural Exchange between Italy
    and the U.S.A.
via Boncompagni, 16
00187 Rome
Italy

APO/FPO OR POUCH ADDRESS:
Educational Advisor
Commission for Educational and Cultural Exchange between Italy
    and the U.S.A.
USIS/American Embassy
APO New York 09794

## *Florence*

INTERNATIONAL MAILING ADDRESS:
Educational Advisor
American Consulate General, USIS
Lungarno Amerigo Vespucci, 46
50123 Florence
Italy

APO/FPO OR POUCH ADDRESS:
Educational Advisor
USIS/Florence
APO New York 09019

## *Genoa*

INTERNATIONAL MAILING ADDRESS:
Educational Advisor
American Consulate General, USIS
Banca d'America e d'Italia Building
Piazza Portello 6
16124 Genoa
Italy

APO/FPO OR POUCH ADDRESS:
Educational Advisor
USIS/Genoa Box G
APO New York 09794

## Milan

INTERNATIONAL MAILING ADDRESS:
Educational Advisor
American Consulate General
via Bigli, 11/A
20121 Milan
Italy
APO/FPO OR POUCH ADDRESS:
Educational Advisor
USIS/Milan Box M
APO New York 09794

## Naples

INTERNATIONAL MAILING ADDRESS:
Educational Advisor
American Studies Center
via Andrea D'Isernia, 36
80122 Naples
Italy
APO/FPO OR POUCH ADDRESS:
Educational Advisor
USIS/Naples
FPO New York 09521

## Palermo

INTERNATIONAL MAILING ADDRESS:
Educational Advisor
American Consulate General, USIS
via Vaccarini, 1
90143 Palermo
Italy
APO/FPO OR POUCH ADDRESS:
Educational Advisor
USIS/Palermo
c/o Amembassy Rome–P
APO New York 09794

## Ivory Coast
### *Abidjan*

INTERNATIONAL MAILING ADDRESS:
Educational Advisor
American Cultural Center
USIS
01 BP 1866
Abidjan 01
Ivory Coast

APO/FPO OR POUCH ADDRESS:
Educational Advisor
USIS/Abidjan
Department of State
Washington, D.C. 20520-2010

## Jamaica
### *Kingston*

INTERNATIONAL MAILING ADDRESS:
Student Counselor
U.S. Information Service
American Embassy
Mutual Life Center
2 Oxford Road
Kingston 5
Jamaica

APO/FPO OR POUCH ADDRESS:
Student Counselor
USIS/Kingston
Department of State
Washington, D.C. 20520-3210

## Japan
### *Tokyo*

INTERNATIONAL MAILING ADDRESS:
Educational Information Service
The Japan–United States Educational Commission
Sanno Grand Building, Room 207
14-2-2 Chome, Nagata-cho
Chiyoda-ku, Tokyo 100
Japan

*Tokyo (continued)*

APO/FPO OR POUCH ADDRESS:
Educational Information Service
Japan-U.S. Educational Commission
c/o USIS/Tokyo
APO San Francisco 96503

# Jerusalem
## *East Jerusalem*

INTERNATIONAL MAILING ADDRESS:
AMIDEAST
P.O. Box 19674
East Jerusalem via Israel

APO/FPO OR POUCH ADDRESS:
PAO
(For Student Counseling Center)
American Consulate General
APO New York 09672

# Jordan
## *Amman*

INTERNATIONAL MAILING ADDRESS:
AMIDEAST
P.O. Box 1249
Amman
Jordan

Educational materials for the following center should be sent through the address listed above:

## *Irbid*

INTERNATIONAL MAILING ADDRESS:
AMIDEAST
Branch Counseling Services
Yarmouk University
Irbid
Jordan

# Kenya
## *Nairobi*

INTERNATIONAL MAILING ADDRESS:
Educational Counseling Office
P.O. Box 45869
Nairobi
Kenya

APO/FPO OR POUCH ADDRESS:
Cultural Affairs Officer
U.S. Embassy
Box 321
APO New York 09675

## *Mombasa*

INTERNATIONAL MAILING ADDRESS:
Educational Advisor
c/o Educational Counseling Office
P.O. Box 45869
Nairobi
Kenya

APO/FPO OR POUCH ADDRESS:
Cultural Affairs Officer
U.S. Embassy
Box 321
APO New York 09675

# Korea
## *Seoul*

INTERNATIONAL MAILING ADDRESS:
Educational Advisor
The Korean-American Educational Commission
Kohap Building, Suite 403
89-4 Kyongun-dong, Chongno-gu
Seoul 110
Korea

APO/FPO OR POUCH ADDRESS:
Cultural Affairs Officer
U.S. Information Service
American Embassy
APO San Francisco 96301

## Kuwait
### *Kuwait*

INTERNATIONAL MAILING ADDRESS:
Educational Advisor
American Embassy/USIS
P.O. Box 77 Safat
13001 Kuwait
Kuwait

APO/FPO OR POUCH ADDRESS:
Educational Advisor
USIS/Kuwait
Department of State
Washington, D.C. 20520-6200

## Lebanon
### *Antelias*

INTERNATIONAL MAILING ADDRESS:
AMIDEAST
P.O. Box 70-744
Antelias
Lebanon

### *Beirut*

INTERNATIONAL MAILING ADDRESS:
AMIDEAST
P.O. Box 135-155
Beirut
Lebanon

## Lesotho
### *Maseru*

INTERNATIONAL MAILING ADDRESS:
American Cultural Center
P.O. Box 573
Maseru
Lesotho
Southern Africa

APO/FPO OR POUCH ADDRESS:
Educational Advisor
USIS/Maseru
Department of State
Washington, D.C. 20520-2340

# Liberia
## *Monrovia*

INTERNATIONAL MAILING ADDRESS:
U.S. Educational and Cultural Foundation in Liberia
P.O. Box 1011
Monrovia
Liberia
West Africa

APO/FPO OR POUCH ADDRESS:
Educational Advisor
U.S. Educational and Cultural Foundation in Liberia
USIS
APO New York 09155

# Madagascar
## *Antananarivo*

INTERNATIONAL MAILING ADDRESS:
Educational Advisor
American Cultural Center
B.P. 620
c/o American Embassy
Antananarivo
Madagascar

APO/FPO OR POUCH ADDRESS:
Educational Advisor
USIS/Antananarivo
Department of State
Washington, D.C. 20520-2040

## Malawi
### *Lilongwe*

INTERNATIONAL MAILING ADDRESS:
Cultural Affairs Specialist
American Cultural Center
P.O. Box 30373
Lilongwe 3
Malawi

APO/FPO OR POUCH ADDRESS:
Cultural Affairs Specialist
USIS/Lilongwe
Department of State
Washington, D.C. 20520-2280

## Malaysia
### *Kuala Lumpur*

INTERNATIONAL MAILING ADDRESS:
Malaysian-American Commission on Educational Exchange
    (MACEE)
355 Jalan Ampang
50450 Kuala Lumpur
Malayasia

APO/FPO OR POUCH ADDRESS:
Director E.I.C.
Malaysian-American Commission on Educational Exchange
    (MACEE)
USIS/Kuala Lumpur
Department of State
Washington, D.C. 20520-4210

### *Penang*

INTERNATIONAL MAILING ADDRESS:
Malaysian-American Commission on Educational Exchange
    (MACEE)
102-B Madras Lane
Penang
Malaysia

## Mali
### *Bamako*

INTERNATIONAL MAILING ADDRESS:
Ambassade Américaine
B.P. 34
Bamako
Mali
West Africa

APO/FPO OR POUCH ADDRESS:
Educational Advisor
USIS/Bamako
Department of State
Washington, D.C. 20520-2050

## Malta
### *Floriana*

INTERNATIONAL MAILING ADDRESS:
Educational Advisor
American Embassy/USIS
P.O. Box 535
Floriana
Malta

APO/FPO OR POUCH ADDRESS:
Educational Advisor
USIS/Valletta
Department of State
Washington, D.C. 20520-5800

## Mauritania
### *Nouakchott*

INTERNATIONAL MAILING ADDRESS:
Educational Advisor
U.S. Embassy
American Cultural Center
B.P. 222
Nouakchott
Mauritania

*Nouakchott (continued)*

APO/FPO OR POUCH ADDRESS:
Educational Advisor
U.S. Embassy/Nouakchott (USIS)
Department of State
Washington, D.C. 20520-2430

## Mauritius
### *Port Louis*

INTERNATIONAL MAILING ADDRESS:
Educational Advisor
USIS/American Embassy
President John Kennedy Street
Port Louis
Mauritius
Indian Ocean

APO/FPO OR POUCH ADDRESS:
Educational Advisor
USIS/Port Louis
Department of State
Washington, D.C. 20520-2450

## Mexico
### *Mexico City*

INTERNATIONAL MAILING ADDRESS:
Institute of International Education (IIE)
Londres 16, 2nd Floor
06600 Mexico, D.F.
Mexico

APO/FPO OR POUCH ADDRESS:
Educational Advisor
Educational Counseling Service
American Embassy
P.O. Box 3087
Laredo, Texas 78041

## Chihuahua

INTERNATIONAL MAILING ADDRESS:
Educational Advisor
Instituto Mexicano-Norteamericano de Relaciones Culturales
Vicente Guerrero 616
3100 Chihuahua, Chihuahua
Mexico

APO/FPO OR POUCH ADDRESS:
Educational Counseling Service
Chihuahua
P.O. Box 10545
Laredo, Texas 78041

## Guadalajara

INTERNATIONAL MAILING ADDRESS:
Educational Advisor
Instituto Cultural Mexicano-Norteamericano de Jaliso
Tolsa 300
Guadalajara, Guadalajara
Mexico

APO/FPO OR POUCH ADDRESS:
Educational Advisor
Educational Counseling Service
Guadalajara
P.O. Box 3088
Laredo, Texas 78041

## Hermosillo

INTERNATIONAL MAILING ADDRESS:
Educational Advisor
Instituto Mexicano-Norteamericano de Relaciones Culturales
Blvd. Navarrete y Monteverde, Valle Hermoso
83260 Hermosillo, Sonora
Mexico

APO/FPO OR POUCH ADDRESS:
Educational Advisor
Educational Counseling Service
Hermosillo
P.O. Box 633
Brownsville, Texas 78522

## *Merida*

INTERNATIONAL MAILING ADDRESS:
Educational Advisor
Instituto Franklin de Yucatán
Calle 57 Num. 474-A
97000 Merida, Yucatán
Mexico

APO/FPO OR POUCH ADDRESS:
Educational Advisor
Educational Counseling Service
Merida
P.O. Box 3087
Laredo, Texas 78041

## *Monterrey*

INTERNATIONAL MAILING ADDRESS:
Instituto Mexicano-Norteamericano de Relaciones Culturales
Hidalgo 768 Pte.
64000 Monterrey, Nuevo León
Mexico

APO/FPO OR POUCH ADDRESS:
Educational Counseling Service
Monterrey
P.O. Box 3098
Laredo, Texas 78041

## *Morelia*

INTERNATIONAL MAILING ADDRESS:
Educational Advisor
Instituto Mexicano-Norteamericano de Relaciones Culturales
Guillermo Prieto 86
5800 Morelia, Michoacán
Mexico

APO/FPO OR POUCH ADDRESS:
Educational Advisor
Educational Counseling Service
Morelia
P.O. Box 3087
Laredo, Texas 78041

## Saltillo

INTERNATIONAL MAILING ADDRESS:
Instituto Mexicano-Norteamericano de Relaciones Culturales
Hildago Nte. 160
2500 Saltillo, Coahuila
Mexico

APO/FPO OR POUCH ADDRESS:
Educational Counseling Service
Saltillo
P.O. Box 3098
Laredo, Texas 78041

## San Luis Potosi

INTERNATIONAL MAILING ADDRESS:
Educational Advisor
Instituto Mexicano-Norteamericano de Relaciones Culturales
avenida Venustiano Carranza 1430
Apartado Postal 567
78250 San Luis Potosi, San Luis Potosi
Mexico

APO/FPO OR POUCH ADDRESS:
Educational Counseling Service
San Luis Potosi
P.O. Box 3087
Laredo, Texas 78041

## Tampico

INTERNATIONAL MAILING ADDRESS:
Educational Advisor
Centro Cultural Mexicano-Americano
Colon 310 Nte.
8900 Tampico, Tamaulipas
Mexico

APO/FPO OR POUCH ADDRESS:
Educational Advisor
Educational Counseling Service
Tampico
P.O. Box 633
Brownsville, Texas 78520

## *Torreón*

INTERNATIONAL MAILING ADDRESS:
Instituto Mexicano-Norteamericano de Relaciones Culturales
Edificio Marcos, 4o. Piso
calle Rodriquez 351 Sur
27150 Torreón, Coahuila
Mexico

APO/FPO OR POUCH ADDRESS:
Educational Counseling Service
Torreón
P.O. Box 3087
Laredo, Texas 78041

## *Veracruz*

INTERNATIONAL MAILING ADDRESS:
Educational Advisor
Instituto Franklin de Veracruz
Azueta 1229 esq. Dian Mirón
91.700 Veracruz, Veracruz
Mexico

APO/FPO OR POUCH ADDRESS:
Educational Advisor
Educational Counseling Service
Veracruz
P.O. Box 3087
Laredo, Texas 78041

## *Zacatecas*

INTERNATIONAL MAILING ADDRESS:
Educational Advisor
Instituto Mexicano-Norteamericano de Relaciones Culturales
Victor Rosales 167, 1er. Piso
98000 Zacatecas, Zacatecas
Mexico

APO/FPO OR POUCH ADDRESS:
Educational Advisor
Educational Counseling Service
Zacatecas
P.O. Box 3087
Laredo, Texas 78041

## Morocco
### *Rabat*

INTERNATIONAL MAILING ADDRESSES:
(Center #1)
Educational Advisor
AMIDEAST
25 bis Patrice Lumumba
Box 8
Rabat
Morocco

(Center #2)
Educational Advisor
American Language Center
4 rue Tanja
Rabat
Morocco

(Center #3)
Educational Advisor
Moroccan-American Commission for Educational and Cultural
    Exchange
3 rue Tiddas
Rabat
Morocco

APO/FPO OR POUCH ADDRESS:
(Center #3)
Educational Advisor
M.A.C.E.C.E.
Rabat-USIS
Department of State
Washington, D.C. 20520-9400

### *Casablanca*

INTERNATIONAL MAILING ADDRESS:
Educational Advisor
American Language Center
1 Place de la Fraternité
Casablanca
Morocco

## Fes

INTERNATIONAL MAILING ADDRESS:
Educational Advisor
American Language Center
Place des États-Unis
Fes
Morocco

## Marrakech

INTERNATIONAL MAILING ADDRESS:
Educational Advisor
American Language Center
3 Impasse Moulin de Gueliz
Marrakech
Morocco

## Tangier

INTERNATIONAL MAILING ADDRESS:
Educational Advisor
American Language Center
P.O. Box 2123
Tangier
Morocco

# Nepal
## Kathmandu

INTERNATIONAL MAILING ADDRESS:
Program Officer
U.S. Educational Foundation in Nepal
Post Box 380
Kathmandu
Nepal

APO/FPO OR POUCH ADDRESS:
Program Officer
U.S. Educational Foundation in Nepal
USIS/Kathmandu
Department of State
Washington, D.C. 20520-6190

# Netherlands
## *Amsterdam*

INTERNATIONAL MAILING ADDRESS:
Student Counselor
Netherlands-American Commission for Educational Exchange
Nieuwe Spiegelstraat 26
1017DG Amsterdam
The Netherlands

APO/FPO OR POUCH ADDRESS:
Student Counselor
Netherlands-American Commission for Educational Exchange
American Embassy/The Hague
APO New York 09159-7041

# Netherlands Antilles
## *Curaçao*

INTERNATIONAL MAILING ADDRESS:
Educational Advisor
American Consulate General
P.O. Box 158
Curaçao
Netherlands Antilles

APO/FPO OR POUCH ADDRESS:
Educational Advisor
USIS/Curaçao
Department of State
Washington, D.C. 20520-3160

# New Zealand
## *Wellington*

INTERNATIONAL MAILING ADDRESS:
Educational Advisor
New Zealand–U.S. Educational Foundation
P.O. Box 3465
Wellington
New Zealand

*Wellington (continued)*

APO/FPO OR POUCH ADDRESS:
Educational Advisor
New Zealand–U.S. Educational Foundation
c/o American Embassy
FPO San Francisco 96690-0001

# Nicaragua
## *Managua*

INTERNATIONAL MAILING ADDRESSES:
(Center #1)
Educational Advisor
American Embassy
Km. 4-½ Carretera Sur
Managua
Nicaragua

(Center #2)
The American-Nicaraguan School
P.O. Box 2670
Managua
Nicaragua

APO/FPO OR POUCH ADDRESS:
(Center #1)
Educational Advisor
USIS/American Embassy
APO Miami 34021

# Niger
## *Niamey*

INTERNATIONAL MAILING ADDRESS:
Educational Advisor
USIS
American Embassy
B.P. 11201
Niamey
Niger

APO/FPO OR POUCH ADDRESS:
Educational Advisor
USIS/Niamey
Department of State
Washington, D.C. 20520-2420

# Nigeria
## *Lagos*

INTERNATIONAL MAILING ADDRESS:
Educational Advisor
USIS
P.O. Box 554
Lagos
Nigeria

APO/FPO OR POUCH ADDRESS:
Educational Advisor
USIS/Lagos
Department of State
Washington, D.C. 20520-8300

## *Kaduna*

INTERNATIONAL MAILING ADDRESS:
Educational Advisor
USIS
P.M.B. 2060
Kaduna, Kaduna State
Nigeria

APO/FPO OR POUCH ADDRESS:
Educational Advisor
USIS/Kaduna
Department of State
Washington, D.C. 20520-2260

# Norway
## *Oslo*

INTERNATIONAL MAILING ADDRESS:
Student Advisor
U.S. Educational Foundation in Norway
Nedre Vollgate 3
0158 Oslo 1
Norway

APO/FPO OR POUCH ADDRESS:
Educational Advisor–Oslo
American Embassy
APO New York 09085

### *Tromso*

INTERNATIONAL MAILING ADDRESS:
Educational Advisor
U.S. Information Office–Tromso
P.O. Box 171
9001 Tromso
Norway

APO/FPO OR POUCH ADDRESS:
Educational Advisor–Tromso
American Embassy/Oslo
APO New York 09085

## Oman
### *Muscat*

INTERNATIONAL MAILING ADDRESS:
Educational Advisor
Embassy of the United States of America (USIS)
P.O. Box 966
Muscat
Oman

APO/FPO OR POUCH ADDRESS:
Educational Advisor
USIS/Muscat
Department of State
Washington, D.C. 20520-6220

## Pakistan
### *Islamabad*

INTERNATIONAL MAILING ADDRESS:
Educational Advisor
U.S. Educational Foundation in Pakistan
P.O. Box 1128
Islamabad
Pakistan

APO/FPO OR POUCH ADDRESS:
Educational Advisor
U.S. Educational Foundation in Pakistan
USIS/Islamabad
Department of State
Washington, D.C. 20520-8100

## *Karachi*

INTERNATIONAL MAILING ADDRESS:
Educational Advisor
Pakistan-American Cultural Center
11-Fatima Jinnah Road
Karachi
Pakistan

APO/FPO OR POUCH ADDRESS:
Educational Advisor
USIS/Karachi
Department of State
Washington, D.C. 20520-6150

## *Lahore*

INTERNATIONAL MAILING ADDRESS:
Educational Advisor
The American Center
20-Fatima Jinnah Road
Lahore
Pakistan

APO/FPO OR POUCH ADDRESS:
Educational Advisor
USIS/Lahore
Department of State
Washington, D.C. 20520-6160

## *Peshawar*

INTERNATIONAL MAILING ADDRESS:
Educational Advisor
The American Center
1-C, Chinar Road
University Town
Peshawar
Pakistan

APO/FPO OR POUCH ADDRESS:
Educational Advisor
USIS/Peshawar
Department of State
Washington, D.C. 20520-6170

## Republic of Panama
### *Panama*

INTERNATIONAL MAILING ADDRESS:
Educational Advisor
Embassy of the United States
P.O. Box 6959
Panama 5
Republic of Panama

APO/FPO OR POUCH ADDRESS:
Educational Advisor
American Embassy
Box E
APO Miami 34002

## Papua New Guinea
### *Port Moresby*

INTERNATIONAL MAILING ADDRESS:
Educational Advisor
American Embassy (USIS)
P.O. Box 1492
Port Moresby
Papua New Guinea

APO/FPO OR POUCH ADDRESS:
Educational Advisor
USIS/Port Moresby
Department of State
Washington, D.C. 20520-4240

## Paraguay
### *Asunción*

INTERNATIONAL MAILING ADDRESS:
Student Counselor
Centro Cultural Paraguayo-Americano
avenida España 352
Asunción
Paraguay

APO/FPO OR POUCH ADDRESS:
Student Counselor
USIS/American Embassy
APO Miami 34036-0001

# Peru
## *Lima*

INTERNATIONAL MAILING ADDRESS:
Educational Advisor
Asesoria Académica
Máximo Abril No. 599
Lima
Peru

APO/FPO OR POUCH ADDRESS:
Educational Advisor
American Embassy (USIS)
APO Miami 34031

## *Arequipa*

INTERNATIONAL MAILING ADDRESS:
Educational Advisor
Instituto Cultural Peruano Norteamericano
Apartado 555
Arequipa
Peru

## *Cuzco*

INTERNATIONAL MAILING ADDRESS:
Educational Advisor
Instituto Cultural Peruano Norteamericano
Apartado 287
Cuzco
Peru

## *Trujillo*

INTERNATIONAL MAILING ADDRESS:
Educational Advisor
Instituto Cultural Peruano Norteamericano
Esq. Husares de Junín y Venezuela
Trujillo
Peru

## Philippines
### *Manila*

INTERNATIONAL MAILING ADDRESS:
The Executive Director
Philippine-American Educational Foundation (PAEF)
P.O. Box 151
Manila
Philippines
APO/FPO OR POUCH ADDRESS:
The Cultural Attaché (PAEF)
American Embassy
APO San Francisco 96528

### *Cebu City*

INTERNATIONAL MAILING ADDRESS:
Educational Advisor
U.S. Information Service
SSS Building, President Osmena Boulevard
Cebu City
Philippines
APO/FPO OR POUCH ADDRESS:
Educational Advisor (USIS)
American Consulate (Cebu)
APO San Francisco 96528

## Poland
### *Warsaw*

INTERNATIONAL MAILING ADDRESS:
Assistant Cultural Attaché for Exchanges
American Embassy
Al. Ujazdowskie 29/31
00-540 Warsaw
Poland
APO/FPO OR POUCH ADDRESS:
Educational Advisor (ACAO-Exchanges)
AM CON GEN (WAW)
APO New York 09213

## Krakow

INTERNATIONAL MAILING ADDRESS:
Branch Public Affairs Officer
American Consulate
Ul. Stolarska 9
31-043 Krakow
Poland

APO/FPO OR POUCH ADDRESS:
Educational Advisor (BPAO)
AM CON GEN (KRA)
APO New York 09213

## Poznan

INTERNATIONAL MAILING ADDRESS:
Branch Public Affairs Officer
American Consulate
Ul. Chopina 4
00-721 Poznan
Poland

APO/FPO OR POUCH ADDRESS:
Educational Advisor (BPAO)
AM CON GEN (POZ)
APO New York 09213

# Portugal
## Lisbon

INTERNATIONAL MAILING ADDRESS:
Educational Advisor
Luso-American Educational Commission
ave. Elias Garcia, 59-5
1000 Lisboa
Portugal

APO/FPO OR POUCH ADDRESS:
Educational Advisor
Luso-American Educational Commission (Fulbright)
USIS/American Embassy
APO New York 09678

## Qatar
### *Doha*

INTERNATIONAL MAILING ADDRESS:
American Embassy
USIS
P.O. Box 2399
Doha
Qatar

APO/FPO OR POUCH ADDRESS:
Educational Advisor
USIS/Doha
Department of State
Washington, D.C. 20520-6130

## Romania
### *Bucharest*

INTERNATIONAL MAILING ADDRESS:
American Embassy
Strada Tudor Arghezi 7-9
Bucharest
Romania

APO/FPO OR POUCH ADDRESS:
Educational Advisor
AM CON GEN (BUCH)
APO New York 09213 (BUH)

## Rwanda
### *Kigali*

INTERNATIONAL MAILING ADDRESS:
Educational Advisor
Ambassade Américaine
B.P. 28
Kigali
Rwanda

APO/FPO OR POUCH ADDRESS:
Educational Advisor
USIS/Kigali
Department of State
Washington, D.C. 20520-2210

## Saudi Arabia
### *Riyadh*

INTERNATIONAL MAILING ADDRESS:
Educational Advisor
American Embassy
Sulaimanniah District
P.O. Box 9041
Riyadh
Saudi Arabia

APO/FPO OR POUCH ADDRESS:
American Embassy
Attn: Educational Advisor
USIS/Riyadh
APO New York 09038

### *Dhahran*

INTERNATIONAL MAILING ADDRESS:
Educational Advisor
American Consulate General
P.O. Box 81
Dhahran Airport
Saudi Arabia

APO/FPO OR POUCH ADDRESS:
Amconsul Dhahran
Attn: Educational Advisor
USIS/Dhahran
APO New York 09616

### *Jidda*

INTERNATIONAL MAILING ADDRESS:
Educational Advisor
American Consulate General
P.O. Box 149
Jidda
Saudi Arabia

APO/FPO OR POUCH ADDRESS:
American Consulate General
Attn: Educational Advisor
USIS/Jidda
APO New York 09697

## Senegal
### *Dakar*

INTERNATIONAL MAILING ADDRESS:
Assistant CAO
American Cultural Center
B.P. 49
Dakar
Senegal

APO/FPO OR POUCH ADDRESS:
Educational Advisor
USIS/Dakar
Department of State
Washington, D.C. 20520-2130

## Seychelles
### *Victoria*

INTERNATIONAL MAILING ADDRESS:
Educational Advisor
American Embassy
Box 251
Victoria, Mahe
Seychelles

APO/FPO OR POUCH ADDRESS:
Educational Advisor
American Embassy
APO New York 09030

## Sierra Leone
### *Freetown*

INTERNATIONAL MAILING ADDRESS:
American Embassy
Corner Walpole and Siaka Stevens Street
Freetown
Sierra Leone

APO/FPO OR POUCH ADDRESS:
Educational Advisor
USIS/Freetown
Department of State
Washington, D.C. 20520-2160

## Singapore
### *Singapore*

INTERNATIONAL MAILING ADDRESS:
Student Counselor
USIS American Library Resource Center
American Embassy
30 Hill Street
Singapore 0617
Singapore

APO/FPO OR POUCH ADDRESS:
Student Counselor
USIS American Library Resource Center
American Embassy
FPO San Francisco 96699-0001

## Somalia
### *Mogadishu*

INTERNATIONAL MAILING ADDRESS:
Educational Advisor
American Embassy, USIS
Box 574
Mogadishu
Somalia
East Africa

APO/FPO OR POUCH ADDRESS:
Educational Advisor, USIS
Amembassy Mogadishu, DOS
Washington, D.C. 20520-2360

## South Africa
### *Pretoria*

INTERNATIONAL MAILING ADDRESS:
Educational Advisor
American Embassy
Southern Life Building
239 Pretorius Street
Pretoria
South Africa

*Pretoria (continued)*

APO/FPO OR POUCH ADDRESS:
Educational Advisor
USIS/Pretoria
Department of State
Washington, D.C. 20520-9300

## Cape Town

INTERNATIONAL MAILING ADDRESS:
Educational Advisor
American Center
P.O. Box 6773
Roggebaai 8012
South Africa

APO/FPO OR POUCH ADDRESS:
Educational Advisor
USIS/Cape Town
Department of State
Washington, D.C. 20520-2480

## Durban

INTERNATIONAL MAILING ADDRESS:
Educational Advisor
American Cultural Center
Durban Bay House
333 Smith Street
4001 Durban
South Africa

APO/FPO OR POUCH ADDRESS:
Educational Advisor
USIS/Durban
Department of State
Washington, D.C. 20520-2490

## *Johannesburg*

INTERNATIONAL MAILING ADDRESS:
Educational Advisor
American Cultural Center
3rd Floor, African Life Building
111 Commissioner Street
2001 Johannesburg
South Africa

APO/FPO OR POUCH ADDRESS:
Educational Advisor
USIS/Johannesburg
Department of State
Washington, D.C. 20520-2500

# Spain
## *Madrid*

INTERNATIONAL MAILING ADDRESS:
Educational Advisor
Commission for Educational Exchange between the U.S.A. and Spain
Paseo del Prado 28, 5th Floor
28014 Madrid
Spain

APO/FPO OR POUCH ADDRESS:
Educational Advisor
Commission for Educational Exchange between the U.S.A. and Spain
USIS/American Embassy
APO New York 09285

## *Barcelona*

INTERNATIONAL MAILING ADDRESS:
Educational Advisor
Instituto de Estudios Norteamericanos
via Augusta 123
08006 Barcelona
Spain

## Sri Lanka
### *Colombo*

INTERNATIONAL MAILING ADDRESS:
Executive Director
United States Educational Foundation in Sri Lanka
American Center Annex
39, Sir Ernest de Silva Mawatha
Colombo 7
Sri Lanka

## Sudan
### *Khartoum*

INTERNATIONAL MAILING ADDRESS:
Educational Advisor
USIS
American Embassy–Khartoum
P.O. Box 699
Khartoum
Sudan

APO/FPO OR POUCH ADDRESS:
Educational Advisor
American Embassy–Khartoum
P.O. Box 120
APO New York 09668

## Suriname
### *Paramaribo*

INTERNATIONAL MAILING ADDRESS:
Educational Advisor
American Embassy
P.O. Box 1821
Paramaribo
Suriname

APO/FPO OR POUCH ADDRESS:
Educational Advisor
USIS/Paramaribo
Department of State
Washington, D.C. 20520-3390

## Swaziland
### *Mbabane*

INTERNATIONAL MAILING ADDRESS:
Educational Advisor
American Embassy
P.O. Box 199
Mbabane
Swaziland

APO/FPO OR POUCH ADDRESS:
Educational Advisor
USIS/Mbabane
Department of State
Washington, D.C. 20520-2350

## Sweden
### *Stockholm*

INTERNATIONAL MAILING ADDRESSES:
(Center #1)
Educational Advisor
Fulbright Commission
Norrmalmstorg 1, Uppg. B. IV
S-111 46 Stockholm
Sweden

(Center #2)
Educational Advisor
Sweden-America Foundation
Box 5280
S-102 46 Stockholm
Sweden

## Switzerland
### *Bern*

INTERNATIONAL MAILING ADDRESS:
Educational Advisor
American Embassy
P.O. Box 1065
CH–3001 Bern
Switzerland

*Bern (continued)*

APO/FPO OR POUCH ADDRESS:
Educational Advisor
USIS/Bern
Department of State
Washington, D.C. 20520-5110

### Zurich

INTERNATIONAL MAILING ADDRESSES:
(Center #1)
Educational Advisor
Swiss-American Students' Exchange
Eth Zentrum, Rektorat
CH–8092 Zurich
Switzerland

(Center #2)
Educational Advisor
Schweizerrische Zentralstelle fuer Hochschulwesen
Sophienstrasse 2
CH–8032 Zurich
Switzerland

## Syria
### Damascus

INTERNATIONAL MAILING ADDRESS:
AMIDEAST
P.O. Box 2313
Damascus
Syria

## Taiwan
### Taipei

INTERNATIONAL MAILING ADDRESS:
Educational Advisor
Foundation for Scholarly Exchange
1-A Chuan Chow Street
Taipei
Taiwan

## Tanzania
### *Dar es Salaam*

INTERNATIONAL MAILING ADDRESS:
Educational Advisor
U.S. Information Service
P.O. Box 9170
Dar es Salaam
Tanzania

APO/FPO OR POUCH ADDRESS:
Educational Advisor
USIS/American Embassy
Dar es Salaam
Department of State
Washington, D.C. 20520-2140

## Thailand
### *Bangkok*

INTERNATIONAL MAILING ADDRESSES:
(Center #1)
Student Advisory Service
USIS
125 South Sathorn Road
Bangkok 10120
Thailand

(Center #2)
Institute of International Education
G.P.O. Box 2050
Bangkok 10501
Thailand

(Center #3)
Educational Advisory Division
P.O. Box 95 B.M.C.
Bangkok 10000
Thailand

(Center #4)
Education Abroad Division
Office of the Civil Service Commission
Pitsanuloke Road
Bangkok 10300
Thailand

*Bangkok (continued)*

APO/FPO OR POUCH ADDRESS:
(Center #1)
Student Advisory Service
Cultural Affairs Office
American Embassy/USIS Box 48
APO San Francisco 96346

# Togo
## *Lome*

INTERNATIONAL MAILING ADDRESS:
Centre Culturel Américain
Box 852
Lome
Togo
West Africa

APO/FPO OR POUCH ADDRESS:
Public Affairs Officer
American Embassy/Lome
Department of State
Washington, D.C. 20520-2300

# Trinidad and Tobago
## *Port of Spain*

INTERNATIONAL MAILING ADDRESS:
Educational Advisor (USIS)
American Embassy
P.O. Box 752
Port of Spain
Trinidad and Tobago

APO/FPO OR POUCH ADDRESS:
Educational Advisor
USIS
American Embassy/Port of Spain
Department of State
Washington, D.C. 20520-3410

## Tunisia
### *Tunis*

INTERNATIONAL MAILING ADDRESS:
Educational Advisor
AMIDEAST
B.P. 1134
Tunis 1045
Tunisia

## Turkey
### *Ankara*

INTERNATIONAL MAILING ADDRESS:
Educational Advisor
Commission for Educational Exchange between the United States
    and Turkey
Sehit Ersan Caddesi No. 28/4
06680 Cankaya, Ankara
Turkey
APO/FPO OR POUCH ADDRESS:
Educational Advisor
USIS/American Embassy
APO New York 09254

### *Istanbul*

INTERNATIONAL MAILING ADDRESS:
Educational Advisor
Commission for Educational Exchange between the United States
    and Turkey
Dumen Sokak No. 3/11
Gumussuyu, Taksim
Istanbul
Turkey
APO/FPO OR POUCH ADDRESS:
Educational Advisor
USIS/American Embassy
APO New York 09254

## Uganda
### *Kampala*

INTERNATIONAL MAILING ADDRESS:
Public Affairs Officer
USIS
P.O. Box 7186
Kampala
Uganda

APO/FPO OR POUCH ADDRESS:
Public Affairs Officer
USIS/Kampala
Department of State
Washington, D.C. 20520-2190

## Union of Soviet Socialist Republics
### *Moscow*

INTERNATIONAL MAILING ADDRESS:
Educational Advisor
American Embassy
Ulitsa Chaykovskogo 19/21/23
Moscow
U.S.S.R.

APO/FPO OR POUCH ADDRESS:
Educational Advisor
American Embassy
APO New York 09862

## United Arab Emirates
### *Abu Dhabi*

INTERNATIONAL MAILING ADDRESS:
Educational Advisor
USIS
American Embassy
P.O. Box 4009
Abu Dhabi
United Arab Emirates

APO/FPO OR POUCH ADDRESS:
Educational Advisor
USIS/Abu Dhabi
Department of State
Washington, D.C. 20520-6010

## *Dubai*

INTERNATIONAL MAILING ADDRESS:
Educational Advisor
USIS, U.S. Consulate
P.O. Box 9343
Dubai
United Arab Emirates

APO/FPO OR POUCH ADDRESS:
Educational Advisor
USIS/Dubai
Department of State
Washington, D.C. 20520-6020

# United Kingdom
## *London*

INTERNATIONAL MAILING ADDRESS:
Fulbright Commission
Educational Advisory Service
6 Porter Street
London, W1M 2HR
United Kingdom

APO/FPO OR POUCH ADDRESS:
Cultural Section
Box 40
USIS/American Embassy/London
FPO New York 09510

## Uruguay
### *Montevideo*

INTERNATIONAL MAILING ADDRESS:
Educational Advisor
Comisión Fulbright
Paraguay 1217
Montevideo
Uruguay

APO/FPO OR POUCH ADDRESS:
Educational Advisor
Commission for Educational Exchange between the U.S.A. and
    Uruguay
USIS/American Embassy
APO Miami 34035


## Venezuela
### *Caracas*

INTERNATIONAL MAILING ADDRESS:
Director
Servicio de Orientación Educacional
Asociación Venezolano-Americana de Amistad
Apartado 60835
Caracas 1060
Venezuela

APO/FPO OR POUCH ADDRESS:
Educational Advisor
USIS/American Embassy
APO Miami 34037


### *Maracaibo*

INTERNATIONAL MAILING ADDRESS:
Asesoria Estudiantil
Centro Venezolano-Americano del Zulia (CEVAZ)
Apartado 419
Ed. Zulia
Maracaibo
Venezuela

APO/FPO OR POUCH ADDRESS:
BPAO
USIS/Maracaibo
APO Miami 34037

# Yemen Arab Republic
## *Sana'a*

INTERNATIONAL MAILING ADDRESS:
AMIDEAST
P.O. Box 1088
Sana'a
Yemen Arab Republic

# Yugoslavia

Educational materials for all centers should be sent through Belgrade's center #1.

## *Belgrade*

INTERNATIONAL MAILING ADDRESSES:
(Center #1)
Educational Advisor
American Center
Cika Ljubina 19
11000 Belgrade
Yugoslavia

(Center #2)
Educational Advisor
Yugoslav-American Commission for Educational Exchange
Trg Marksa I Engelsa 1
11000 Belgrade
Yugoslavia

APO/FPO OR POUCH ADDRESS:
(Center #1)
USIS/Belgrade
Department of State
Washington, D.C. 20520-5070

## *Ljubljana*

INTERNATIONAL MAILING ADDRESS:
Educational Advisor
American Center
Cankarjeva 11
61000 Ljubljana
Yugoslavia

## Sarajevo

INTERNATIONAL MAILING ADDRESS:
Educational Advisor
American Center
Kranjcevica A-3
71000 Sarajevo
Yugoslavia

## Skopje

INTERNATIONAL MAILING ADDRESS:
Educational Advisor
American Center
Gradski Zid, Blok IV
91000 Skopje
Yugoslavia

## Titograd

INTERNATIONAL MAILING ADDRESS:
Educational Advisor
American Center
Bulevar Oktobarske Revolucije 100
81000 Titograd
Yugoslavia

## Zagreb

INTERNATIONAL MAILING ADDRESS:
Educational Advisor
American Consulate General
Brace Kavurica 2
41000 Zagreb
Yugoslavia

## Zaire
### *Kinshasa*

INTERNATIONAL MAILING ADDRESS:
Educational Advisor
American Embassy, Kinshasa
Building Commimmo
boulevard du 30 Juin
B.P. 8622
Kinshasa 1
Zaire

APO/FPO OR POUCH ADDRESS:
Educational Advisor
USIS/American Embassy, Kinshasa 1
APO New York 09662

## Zambia
### *Lusaka*

INTERNATIONAL MAILING ADDRESS:
The American Center
P.O. Box 32053
Lusaka
Zambia

APO/FPO OR POUCH ADDRESS:
Educational Advisor
USIS/Lusaka
Department of State
Washington, D.C. 20520-2310

## Zimbabwe
### *Harare*

INTERNATIONAL MAILING ADDRESS:
Educational Advisor
U.S. Information Service
P.O. Box 4010
Harare
Zimbabwe

*Harare (continued)*

**APO/FPO OR POUCH ADDRESS:**
Educational Advisor
USIS/Harare
Department of State
Washington, D.C. 20520-2180